ITALIAN DINNER PARTY

WITH FRIENDS

TANJA ARIENZALE

EASY ITALIAN RECIPES
TO SHARE WITH FRIENDS
WITHOUT TIRESOME HOURS IN THE KITCHEN

TABLE OF CONTENTS

INTRODUCTION

BENVENUTI! WELCOME TO "ITALIAN DINNER PARTY WITH FRIENDS". IN THIS COOKBOOK, WE INVITE YOU TO EMBARK ON A DELECTABLE EXPEDITION THROUGH THE RICH TAPESTRY OF ITALIAN CUISINE. PICTURE YOURSELF GATHERED AROUND A TABLE WITH LOVED ONES, IMMERSED IN THE WARMTH OF FRIENDSHIP AND THE TANTALIZING AROMAS WAFTING FROM THE KITCHEN. HERE, AMIDST LAUGHTER AND LIVELY CONVERSATION, FOOD TAKES CENTER STAGE, WEAVING TOGETHER STORIES OF TRADITION, CULTURE, AND PASSION.

ITALY'S CULINARY HERITAGE IS AS DIVERSE AS ITS LANDSCAPES, WITH EACH REGION BOASTING ITS OWN UNIQUE FLAVORS AND SPECIALTIES. FROM THE SUN-DRENCHED SHORES OF SICILY TO THE MISTY HILLS OF TUSCANY, OUR JOURNEY WILL TRAVERSE THE LENGTH AND BREADTH OF THIS GASTRONOMIC PARADISE. ALONG THE WAY, YOU'LL DISCOVER THE SECRETS OF AUTHENTIC ITALIAN COOKING, PASSED DOWN THROUGH GENERATIONS AND CHERISHED IN EVERY HOUSEHOLD...

AT THE HEART OF ITALIAN CUISINE LIES A REVERENCE FOR SIMPLICITY AND QUALITY INGREDIENTS. WHETHER IT'S A RUSTIC PASTA DISH, A SUCCULENT ROAST, OR A DELICATE RISOTTO, THE FOCUS IS ALWAYS ON LETTING THE NATURAL FLAVOURS SHINE. WITH OUR RECIPES, WE AIM TO CAPTURE THE ESSENCE OF ITALIAN COOKING WHILE OFFERING A CONTEMPORARY TWIST THAT IS ACCESSIBLE TO HOME COOKS OF ALL SKILL LEVELS.

BUT "ITALIAN DINNER PARTY WITH FRIENDS" IS MORE THAN JUST A COLLECTION OF RECIPES; IT'S AN INVITATION TO CELEBRATE THE JOY OF SHARED MEALS AND THE BONDS THAT ARE FORGED OVER FOOD. WHETHER YOU'RE PLANNING A COZY DINNER FOR TWO OR HOSTING A LIVELY GATHERING OF FRIENDS AND FAMILY, OUR DISHES ARE DESIGNED TO BRING PEOPLE TOGETHER AND CREATE UNFORGETTABLE CULINARY EXPERIENCES.

SO, JOIN US AS WE EXPLORE THE VIBRANT MOSAIC OF ITALIAN CUISINE. FROM ANTIPASTI TO DOLCI, EACH RECIPE IS A CELEBRATION OF ITALY'S CULINARY HERITAGE AND A TRIBUTE TO THE ENDURING PLEASURE OF DINING WITH FRIENDS.

BUON APPETITO!

SECTION 1

APERITIVO

APERITIVO INTRODUCTION

YOU HAVE PROBABLY THROWN THE WORD APERITIVO AROUND ONCE OR TWICE, OR SEEN IT ON NUMEROUS MENU'S. APERITIVO IS AN ITALIAN WORD USED TO DESCRIBE A COCKTAIL AND THE ITALIAN HAPPY HOUR. IT IS A PRE-MEAL DRINK; APERITIVO IN ITALY IS A CULTURAL RITUAL. IT COMES FROM THE LATIN WORD APERIRE, MEANING "TO OPEN" THE STOMACH BEFORE DINING.

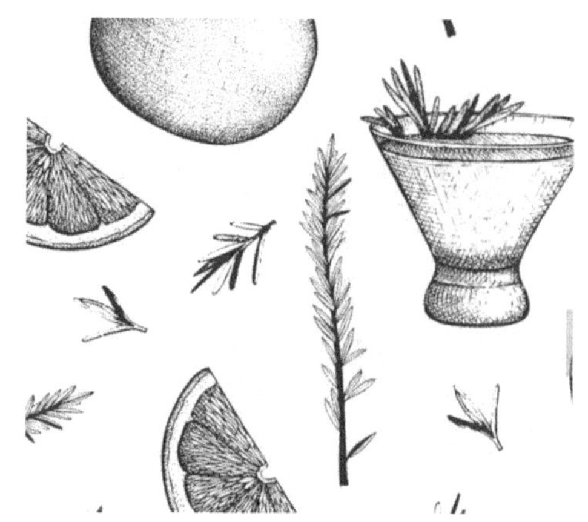

SPRITZ WITH A TWIST

SERVES: 4   PREP TIME: 5 MIN   TOTAL TIME: 8 MIN

INGREDIENTS

- 4 X LOWBALL OR WINE GLASSES
- ICE CUBES
- APEROL
- PROSECCO
- JUICE FROM ONE WHOLE LIME
- A SPLASH OF SPARKLING WATER
- GRAPEFRUIT WEDGE
- ROSEMARY FOR GARNISH

INSTRUCTIONS

1. ADD 3-4 CUBES OF ICE INTO EACH GLASS
2. POUR 40ML OF APEROL IN EACH GLASS OVER THE ICE FOLLOWED BY 60ML OF PROSECCO
3. ADD A DASH OF LIME JUICE
4. GIVE IT A STIR
5. THEN ADD A SPLASH OF SPARKLING WATER
6. ADD A WEDGE OF GRAPEFRUIT INTO THE GLASS
7. ADD ROSEMARY FOR GARNISH

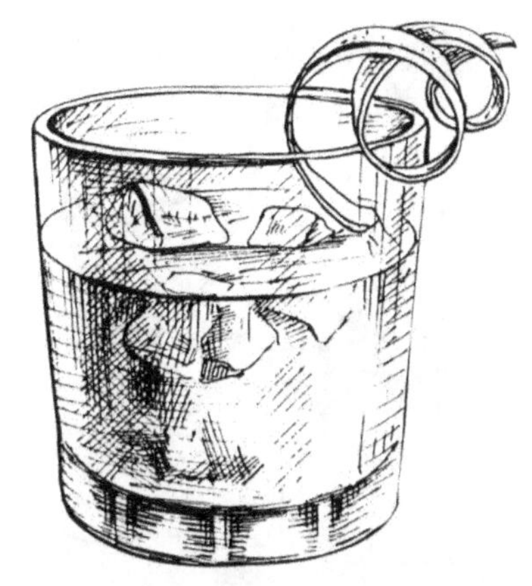

NEGRONI'S WITH HOMIES

SERVES: 4   PREP TIME: 5 MIN   TOTAL TIME: 8 MIN

INGREDIENTS

- 4 X TUMBLERS
- HIGH QUALITY GIN
- SWEET VERMOUTH
- CAMPARI
- ICE
- SLICE OF ORANGE TO GARNISH

INSTRUCTIONS

1. POUR 100ML GIN, 100ML VERMOUTH AND 100ML CAMPARI INTO A MIXING GLASS OR JUG WITH ICE. STIR WELL UNTIL THE OUTSIDE OF THE GLASS FEELS COLD.

1. STRAIN 75ML OF THE MIXTURE INTO EACH TUMBLER AND ADD 1 LARGE ICE SPHERE OR SOME FRESH ICE, AND GARNISH WITH AN ORANGE SLICE, USING A BLOOD ORANGE WHEN IN SEASON.

NEGRONI SBAGLIATO

SERVES: 4   PREP TIME: 5 MIN   TOTAL TIME: 8 MIN

INGREDIENTS

- 4 X FLUTES OR TUMBLERS
- PROSECCO
- SWEET VERMOUTH
- CAMPARI
- ICE
- SLICE OF ORANGE TO GARNISH

INSTRUCTIONS

1. POUR 100ML VERMOUTH AND 100ML CAMPARI INTO A MIXING GLASS OR JUG WITH ICE. STIR WELL UNTIL THE OUTSIDE OF THE GLASS FEELS COLD.

1. STRAIN 50ML OF THE MIXTURE INTO EACH GLASS AND ADD 1 LARGE ICE SPHERE OR SOME FRESH ICE.

1. TOP UP WITH 25ML OF PROSECCO (OR AS MUCH AS YOU WANT) AND GARNISH WITH AN ORANGE SLICE OR BLOOD ORANGE WHEN IN SEASON.

BELLINI OR ROSSINI

SERVES: 4+   PREP TIME: 5 MIN   TOTAL TIME: 8 MIN

INGREDIENTS

BBELLINI
- **PROSECCO**
- **PEACH PUREE (YOU CAN MARINATE PEACHES IN WINE TO BE EXTRA FANCY)**

ROSSINI
- **PROSECCO**
- **STRAWBERRY PUREE (BLEND FRESH STRAWBERRIES IF YOU CAN)**

INSTRUCTIONS

1. **POUR A DASH OF PEACH PUREE OR STRAWBERRY PUREE INTO THE BOTTOM OF A FLUTE**

1. **TOP WITH YOUR FAVOURITE PROSECCO**

A BEAUTIFUL BRUNCH, LUNCH OR PRE-DINNER DRINK

AMERICANO ITALIANO

SERVES: 4+   PREP TIME: 5 MIN   TOTAL TIME: 8 MIN

INGREDIENTS

- **GLASS TUMBLER OR HIGHBALL**
- **2 TABLESPOONS CAMPARI**
- **2 TABLESPOONS SWEET VERMOUTH**
- **60ML SODA WATER**
- **FOR THE GARNISH: LEMON OR ORANGE WEDGE**

INSTRUCTIONS

1. **IN YOUR CHOSENGLASS, STIR TOGETHER THE CAMPARI AND VERMOUTH. ADD ICE AND TOP WITH SODA WATER.**

1. **STIR LIGHTLY AND GARNISH WITH A LEMON OR ORANGE WEDGE.**

GIN AND IT

INGREDIENTS

- JIGGER SHOT UTENSIL
- COCKTAIL GLASS IF AVAILABLE
- 3/4 SHOT SWEET VERMOUTH
- 1 1/2 SHOTS GIN
- 1 OR 3 MARASCHINO CHERRIES, FOR GARNISH

INSTRUCTIONS

1. POUR THE VERMOUTH DIRECTLY INTO A COCKTAIL GLASS WITHOUT ICE.
2. ADD THE GIN
3. GARNISH WITH CHERRIES. IF YOU PREFER CHILLED COCKTAILS, STIR IT WITH ICE IN A MIXING GLASS AND STRAIN IT INTO A COCKTAIL GLASS. ENJOY.

*SOME RECIPES ADD A DASH OF ORANGE BITTERS, WHICH IS ADVISABLE IF THESE ARE THE KIND OF FLAVORS YOU GRAVITATE TOWARD WHEN ORDERING A COCKTAIL.

*THE ODD NUMBER OF CHERRIES SUGGESTED IS NOT JUST A RANDOM CHOICE. TRADITIONALLY, YOU SHOULD USE EITHER ONE OR THREE CHERRIES, NEVER AN EVEN NUMBER AS IT'S BELIEVED TO BRING BAD LUCK.

SECTION 2

ANTIPASTO

THE TERM ANTIPASTO MEANS "BEFORE THE MEAL." IN ITALY THIS STARTER CAN BE AS SIMPLE AS A BOWL OF OLIVES, A PLATTER OF ASSORTED CURED MEATS, CHEESES, VEGETABLES. IT CAN ALSO BE SMALL-BITE APPETIZERS, LITTLE DISHES MEANT TO AWAKEN THE SENSES WITHOUT SPOILING THE APPETITE. ANTIPASTO PRESENTATIONS ARE GENERALLY COLORFUL AND BOAST MANY DIVERSE ITEMS, TO GET PEOPLE EXCITED FOR THE MEAL.

ANTIPASTI PLATE

SERVES: 6   PREP TIME: 15 MIN   TOTAL TIME: 15 MIN

INGREDIENTS

- 2 X LARGE MOZZARELLA BALLS , TORN IN HALF
- 1 RED CHILLI , DESEEDED AND FINELY CHOPPED
- 20 SLICES QUALITY PROSCIUTTO/BRESAOLA/SALAMI
- 280G ARTICHOKES IN OLIVE OIL, DRAINED, RESERVE OIL
- 300G SUNDRIED TOMATOES IN OLIVE OIL, DRAINED, RESERVE OIL
- 290G BALSAMIC SUNDRIED PEPPERS IN OIL, DRAINED, RESERVE OIL
- 3 TABLESPOONS MIXED OLIVES
- 1 HANDFUL CHERRY TOMATOES , HALVED
- PARMESAN, FOR SHAVING
- 20G FRESH BASIL , LEAVES PICKED
- 1 LOAF CIABATTA BREAD, SLICED

INSTRUCTIONS

- PLACE THE MOZZARELLA AT THE EDGES OF A LARGE PLATE AND SCATTER WITH CHILLI.
- ARRANGE THE CURED MEAT AND ALL THE VEGETABLES IN SMALL PILES OVER THE REST OF THE PLATE. TOP THE MEAT WITH SOME PARMESAN.
- PUT MOST OF THE BASIL LEAVES IN A PESTLE AND MORTAR WITH A PINCH OF SALT AND CRUSH TO A PASTE.
- ADD A FEW TABLESPOONS OF THE RESERVED OLIVE OIL FROM THE JARS AND STIR TO MAKE A BASIL-FLAVOURED OIL. SPOON IT OVER THE MOZZARELLA AND THE VEGETABLES, THEN DRIZZLE WITH A LITTLE OLIVE OIL.
- TOAST THE CIABATTA, DRIZZLE WITH A BIT MORE OF THE RESERVED OIL AND SERVE EVERYTHING TOGETHER WITH THE REMAINING BASIL LEAVES SCATTERED OVER.

Radicchio

RADICCHIO CITRUS SALAD

SERVES: 8   PREP TIME: 10 MIN   TOTAL TIME: 20 MIN

INGREDIENTS

- 4 MEDIUM-SIZE BLOOD ORANGES OR ORANGES
- 2 MEDIUM SHALLOTS, THINLY SLICED
- ¼ CUP SHERRY VINEGAR
- 1 TEASPOON HONEY
- ½ TEASPOON SEA SALT
- 1 LARGE HEAD PINK RADICCHIO TRIMMED AND LEAVES SEPARATED
- 1 LARGE FENNEL CUT IN ½ AND THINLY SLICED
- 1 TEASPOON FLAKY SEA SALT, PLUS MORE TO TASTE
- ½ TEASPOON BLACK PEPPER
- 1 CUP PARMIGIANO-REGGIANO CHEESE, SHAVED

INSTRUCTIONS

1. JUICE 1 ORANGE TO GET 1/4 CUP ORANGE JUICE. STIR TOGETHER JUICE, SHALLOTS, SHERRY VINEGAR, HONEY, AND HALF THE SALT IN A SMALL BOWL. LEAVE FOR ABOUT 10 MINUTES.
2. MEANWHILE, CAREFULLY REMOVE PEELS FROM REMAINING 3 ORANGES, USING A SHARP KNIFE TO CUT ALONG THE CURVE OF EACH ORANGE, REMOVING AS LITTLE FLESH AS POSSIBLE; DISCARD PEELS. SLICE PEELED ORANGES CROSSWISE INTO 1/2-INCH-THICK ROUNDS, SET ASIDE.
3. PLACE PINK RADICCHIO LEAVES AND FENNEL IN A LARGE BOWL. POUR ORANGE JUICE MIXTURE OVER RADICCHIO LEAVES, TOSS THOROUGHLY USING YOUR HANDS. ADD ORANGE ROUNDS, FLAKY SEA SALT, AND 1/4 TEASPOON PEPPER; GENTLY TOSS. SEASON WITH ADDITIONAL FLAKY SEA SALT TO TASTE. TOP EVENLY WITH CHEESE AND REMAINING 1/4 TEASPOON PEPPER.

CAPRESE SALAD

SERVES: 4   PREP TIME: 10 MIN TOTAL TIME: 15 MIN

INGREDIENTS

- 3 RIPE GOOD QUALITY TOMATOES
- 1 PUNNET CHERRY TOMATOES
- JUICE OF 1 LEMON
- PINCH OF OREGANO
- BALSAMIC VINEGAR
- EXTRA VIRGIN OLIVE OIL
- TWO HANDFULS OF BASIL LEAVES
- 8 PIECES OF BUFFALO MOZZARELLA TORN INTO PIECES
- 200ML SHEEP'S YOGHURT (OPTIONAL)
- SALT & PEPPER

INSTRUCTIONS

- SLICE TOMATOES INTO 1/2 CM DISCS AND ARRANGE ON THE PLATE

- CUT ALL CHERRY TOMATOES IN HALF

- IN A BOWL, COMBINE YOGHURT (IF USING), LEMON JUICE, OREGANO, VINEGAR, OIL, BASIL AND MOZZARELLA, AND HALVED CHERRY TOMATOES, SEASON WITH SALT & PEPPER.

- ARRANGE MIXTURE OVER SLICED TOMATOES AND ADD MORE PEPPER IF DESIRED.

BRUSCHETTA 3 WAYS

SERVES: 4   PREP TIME: 10 MIN   TOTAL TIME: 20 MIN

INGREDIENTS

- 1 X LARGE LOAF OF SOURDOUGH BREAD SLICED THICK & TOASTED
- EXTRA VIRGIN OLIVE OIL
- SALT + PEPPER

EGGPLANT + MINT
- 2 MEDIUM EGGPLANT, SLICED 3MM THIN
- HANDFUL FLATLEAF PARSLEY
- HANDFUL OF MINT
- 1 CLOVE GARLIC PEELED AND THINLY SLICED

TOMATO + BASIL
- HANDFUL OF MIXED RIPE TOMATOES
- BUNCH OF BASIL

ARTICHOKE + GARLIC
- JAR OF BABY ARTICHOKE (HIGH QUALITY)
- 4 GARLIC CLOVES CHOPPED
- HANDFUL MINT
- HALF LEMON

INSTRUCTIONS

EGGPLANT + MINT
- HEAT A GRIDDLE PAN UTIL HOT. LAY EGGPLANT SIDE BY SIDE UNTIL NICELY CHARRED.
- WHILE THEY ARE GRILLING PUT 8 TBSP OLIVE OIL, 3 TBSP VINEGAR WITH PARSLEY, MINT & GARLIC, SEASON WITH SALT & PEPPER.
- WHEN EGGPLANT IS DONE, ADD THEM TO DRESSING, MIX AND PLACE ON TOASTED SLICED SOURDOUGH. PRESS DOWN.

TOMATO + BASIL
- WASH TOMATOES, REMOVE THEIR CORES, CAREFULLY SQUEEZE SEEDS OUT, CHOP CHUNKY OR FINE.
- PLACE TOMATOES IN A BOWL, TEAR THE BASIL, SEASON WITH SALT, PEPPER & OLIVE OIL & VINEGAR. SCRUNCH THEM IN YOUR FINGERS AND PLACE ONTO TOAST.

ARTICHOKE + GARLIC
- STRAIN ARTICHOKES THEN POP THEM INTO A PAN WITH GARLIC FOR 4 MINS UNTIL GOLDEN.
- SQUEEZE IN A LITTLE LEMON JUICE, ADD MINT, SALT & PEPPER. MASH HALF, SPREAD ONTO TOAST AND RESERVE REST FOR THE TOPPING. ADD PARMESAN IF DESIRED.

FUNGHI CON MOZZARELLA

SERVES: 4   PREP TIME: 10 MIN TOTAL TIME: 20 MIN

INGREDIENTS

- 2 BIG HANDFULLS OF MUSHROOMS VERY THINLY SLICED
- 2 X 150G BALLS OF MOZZARELLA CHEESE TORN INTO SMALL PIECES
- SPRIG OF FRESH THYME, PICK THE LEAVES
- SALT & PEPPER
- EXTRA VIRGIN OLIVE OIL
- CRUSTY BREAD

INSTRUCTIONS

- GRAB AN OVENPROOF PLATTER AND SPREAD THE THINLY SLICED MUSHROOMS ON IT IN ONE LAYER

- SCATTER OVER THE CHEESE AND THYME LEAVES.

- SEASON WITH SALT, PEPPER & OLIVE OIL

- PLACE PLATE UNDER THE GRILL FOR A COUPLE OF MINUTES, CHECKING FREQUENTLY

- ONCE CHEESE IS MELTED AND BUBBLING TUCK IN WITH SOME CRUSTY BREAD

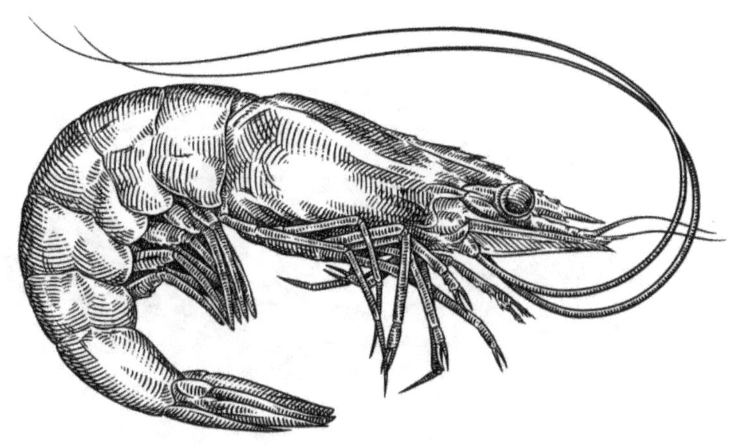

KING PRAWNS GARLIC + CHILLI

SERVES: 4   PREP TIME: 5 MIN   TOTAL TIME: 10 MIN

INGREDIENTS

- EXTRA VIRGIN OLIVE OIL
- 12 FRESH RAW KING PRAWNS, SHELLS ON
- 6 GARLIC CLOVES
- 1 LARGE RED CHILLI
- HANDFUL FLAT LEAF PARSLEY
- 250ML WHITE WINE
- 1 LEMON CUT INTO WEDGES

INSTRUCTIONS

- HEAT THE OIL IN LARGE FRYING PAN, ADD THE KING PRAWNS AND COOK FOR 2 MINS TURNING ONCE.

- ADD THE GARLIC & CHILLI, SEASON WITH SALT, THEN REDUCE THE HEAT AND COOK FOR A COUPLE OF MINUTES WITH A LID ON.

- ADD THE PARSLEY, INCREASE THE HEAT AND ADD THE WINE.

- BUBBLE UNTIL EVAPORATED THEN SERVE IMMEDIATELY WITH LEMON WEDGES AND GOOD QUALITY BREAD TO SCARPETTA (MOP UP SAUCE)

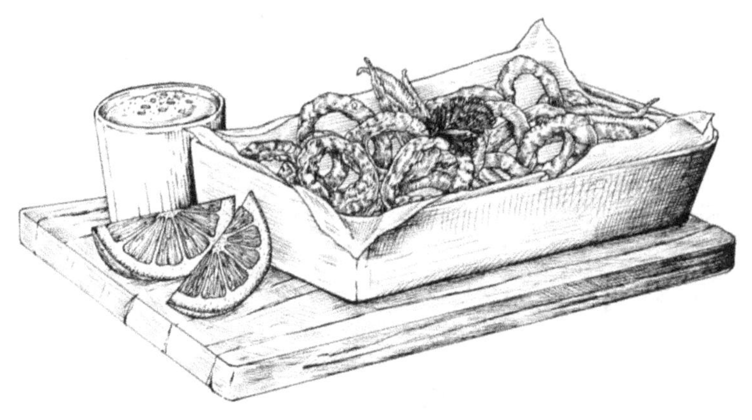

BRAISED CALAMARI

SERVES: 4   PREP TIME: 10 MIN TOTAL TIME: 45 MIN

INGREDIENTS

- 1 KG SQUID CLEANED AND CHOPPED INTO QUARTERS
- EXTRA VIRGIN OLIVE OIL
- 6 ANCHOVY FILLETS
- 10G CAPERS
- 2 GARLIC CLOVES SLICED
- 1 CHILLI CLEANED AND CHOPPED
- 50ML WHITE WINE
- SALT
- 250G CHERRY TOMATOES HALVED
- HANDFUL OF FLATLEAF PARSLEY

INSTRUCTIONS

- HEAT THE OIL IN A SAUCEPAN, ADD THE ANCHOVIES & CAPERS. COOK OVER MEDIUM HEAT. STIRRING UNTIL ANCHOVIES DISSOLVE.
- ADD GARLIC, CHILLI, STIR AND COOK FOR A COUPLE MORE MINUTES.
- ADD THE SQUID AND A PINCH OF SALT AND STIR FRY FOR A FEW MINUTES.
- ADD THE WINE AND BOIL UNTIL IT EVAPORATES.
- ADD CHERRY TOMATOES & PARSLEY, REDUCE HEAT TO LOW AND COOK FOR 45MINS.
- REMOVE FROM HEAT AND SERVE...WITH BREAD OF COURSE.

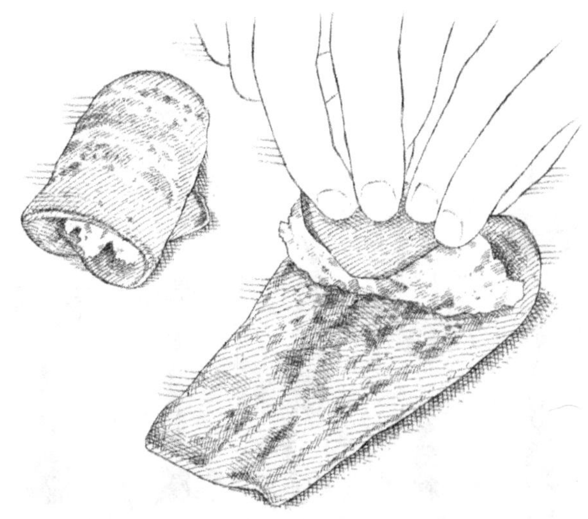

EGGPLANT INVOLTINI (GF)

SERVES: 6   PREP TIME: 5 MIN   TOTAL TIME: 25 MIN

INGREDIENTS

- 3 LONG AUBERGINES/EGGPLANT
- OLIVE OIL
- 50G PINE NUTS
- 6 SUNDRIED TOMATOES IN OIL
- 3 ANCHOVIES IN OIL, FROM SUSTAINABLE SOURCES
- EXTRA VIRGIN OLIVE OIL
- ½ A BUNCH OF FRESH BASIL
- 10 SLICES OF PARMA HAM
- 2 X 125G BALLS OF MOZZARELLA CHEESE

INSTRUCTIONS

- SLICE THE AUBERGINES/EGGPLANTS LONGWAYS INTO ½CM-PIECES, TRIMMING THE SKIN FROM THE OUTER PIECES TO GIVE YOU FLAT FINISHES ON BOTH SIDES, THEN BRUSH THEM WITH 2 TABLESPOONS OF OLIVE OIL.
- HEAT A GRIDDLE PAN ON HIGH HEAT, ONCE HOT, GRIDDLE THE AUBERGINE SLICES FOR 3 MINUTES ON EACH SIDE, UNTIL CHARRED, SET ASIDE.
- TOAST THE PINE NUTS IN A DRY FRYING PAN, THEN TRANSFER TO A FOOD PROCESSOR WITH THE SUNDRIED TOMATOES, ANCHOVIES AND GENEROUS SPLASH OF EXTRA VIRGIN OLIVE OIL. PICK IN MOST OF THE BASIL LEAVES.
- BLITZ UNTIL YOU HAVE A SPREADABLE PASTE, THEN SEASON WITH BLACK PEPPER AND PULSE AGAIN TO COMBINE.
- LAY A SLICE OF PARMA HAM ON TOP OF EACH AUBERGINE STRIP, TEARING OFF THE EXCESS TO USE AGAIN, AND SPREAD ON A LITTLE SUNDRIED TOMATO PASTE.
- TEAR THE MOZZARELLA INTO BITE-SIZED PIECES, THEN PLACE A PIECE AT ONE END OF THE STRIP ALONG WITH A BASIL LEAF. ROLL UP AND SECURE WITH A TOOTH PICK. SERVE IMMEDIATELY.

DIY FORK FINGER FOOD

SERVES: AS MANY AS YOU WANT **PREP TIME: 5 MIN** **TOTAL TIME: 5 MIN**

INGREDIENTS

- **ENGLISH MUSTARD**
- **BRESAOLA (ITALIAN CURED BEEF)**
- **COLESLAW**
- **CORNICHONS**
- **EXTRA VIRGIN OLIVE OIL**
- **LEMON JUICE**

- **FIGS OR ROCKMELON**
- **BUFFALO MOZZARELLA**
- **MINT LEAVES**
- **QUALITY PARMA HAM OR PROSCIUTTO**
- **EXTRA VIRGIN OLIVE OIL**
- **BALSAMIC VINEGAR**

INSTRUCTIONS

BRESAOLA WITH SLAW
- SIMPLY SMEAR A LITTLE ENGLISH MUSTARD COVER A SLICE OF BRESAOLA THEN ADD A PINCH OF COLESLAW IN THE MIDDLE. POP A FEW CORNICHONS ON TOP THEN STAB ON YOUR FORK AND FINISH WITH A TINY DRIZZLE OF EXTRA VIRGIN OLIVE OIL AND A GOOD SQUEEZE OF LEMON JUICE.

PARMA HAM STARTERS
- QUARTER A FIG OR MELON, PINCH APART SOME BUFFALO MOZZARELLA, TAKE A MINT LEAF THEN WRAP A SLICE OF PARMA HAM OR PROSCIUTTO AROUND EVERYTHING & STAB TOGETHER ON YOUR FORK. DRIZZLE A LITTLE EXTRA VIRGIN OLIVE OIL & BALSAMIC VINEGAR. THIS COMBINATION IS FRESH AND LOVELY.

BUFFALO MOZZARELLA WITH FIG

SERVES: 4   PREP TIME: 5 MIN   TOTAL TIME: 5 MIN

INGREDIENTS

- 400G BUFFALO MOZZARELLA, DRAINED
- 10 THIN SLICES PROSCIUTTO
- 4 FRESH FIGS, HALVED
- HONEY, TO DRIZZLE
- OLIVE OIL, TO DRIZZLE
- BABY HERBS, TO SPRINKLE (OPTIONAL)

INSTRUCTIONS

- ARRANGE THE MOZZARELLA, PROSCIUTTO AND FIG ON A PLATE OR PLATTER. DRIZZLE WITH HONEY AND OIL, AND SPRINKLE WITH HERBS.

IT IS THAT SIMPLE!!!

SECTION 3

PASTA, PIZZA, GNOCCHI & RISOTTO

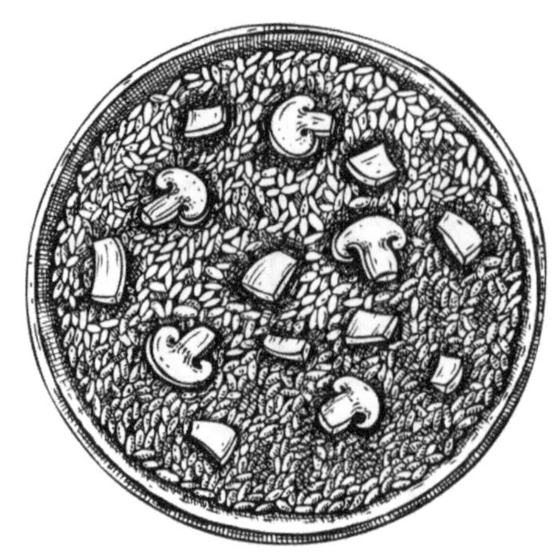

MUSHROOM RISOTTO

SERVES: 6   PREP TIME: 5 MIN   TOTAL TIME: 45 MIN

INGREDIENTS

- 1.1 LITRES (2 PINTS) ORGANIC STOCK (ANY FLAVOUR)
- 1 LARGE ONION
- 2 CLOVES OF GARLIC
- 4 OR 5 STICKS OF CELERY
- HANDFUL THYME SPRIGS
- OLIVE OIL
- 4 HANDFULS OF WILD MIXED MUSHROOMS
- 70G BUTTER , PLUS 1 EXTRA KNOB FOR FRYING
- 400G RISOTTO RICE
- 2 GLASSES OF DRY WHITE WINE
- 115G PARMESAN CHEESE

INSTRUCTIONS

- SLICE MUSHROOMS AND PUT IN OVEN TO ROAST FOR 30MINS WITH FRESH THYME SPRIGS, SALT, PEPPER AND OLIVE OIL.
- PEEL AND FINELY CHOP THE ONION AND GARLIC. TRIM AND FINELY CHOP THE CELERY.
- PUT 2 TBLS OF OLIVE OIL AND A KNOB OF BUTTER INTO A SEPARATE PAN, ADD ONION, GARLIC AND CELERY, AND COOK VERY SLOWLY FOR ABOUT 15 MINUTES WITHOUT COLOURING. WHEN THE VEGETABLES HAVE SOFTENED, ADD THE RICE AND TURN UP THE HEAT.
- KEEP STIRRING UNTIL THE RICE LOOKS SLIGHTLY TRANSLUCENT. ADD THE WINE AND KEEP STIRRING. THE ALCOHOL SMELL WILL EVAPORATE.
- ONCE THE WINE HAS COOKED INTO THE RICE, ADD YOUR FIRST CUP OF HOT STOCK AND A GOOD PINCH OF SEA SALT. TURN THE HEAT DOWN TO A SIMMER. KEEP ADDING THE STOCK AS THE RICE ABSORBS IT, KEEP STIRRING. THIS WILL TAKE AROUND 15 MINUTES.
- TASTE THE RICE TO CHECK IF IT'S COOKED. IF NOT, CARRY ON ADDING STOCK UNTIL THE RICE IS SOFT BUT WITH A SLIGHT BITE. DON'T FORGET TO CHECK THE SEASONING CAREFULLY. IF YOU RUN OUT OF STOCK BEFORE THE RICE IS COOKED, ADD SOME BOILING WATER.
- REMOVE FROM THE HEAT AND ADD THE 70G BUTTER AND ROASTED MUSHROOMS. GRATE IN THE PARMESAN. STIR WELL. PLACE A LID ON THE PAN AND ALLOW TO SIT FOR 2 MINUTES. THEN DISH BIG SPOONFULS ONTO EACH PLATE AND GIVE THE PLATE A TAP UNDERNEATH TO ALLOW THE RISOTTO TO FLATTEN. GRATE MORE PARMESAN ON EACH SERVING AND SPRINKLE THYME AND PEPPER IF DESIRED.

PRAWN RISOTTO

SERVES: 6   PREP TIME: 10 MIN   TOTAL TIME: 40 MIN

INGREDIENTS

- 1 CUP ARBORIO RICE
- 450G LARGE UNCOOKED PRAWNS, PEELED AND DEVEINED
- 4 CUPS CHICKEN OR VEGETABLE BROTH, KEPT WARM
- 1 SMALL ONION, FINELY CHOPPED
- 2 CLOVES GARLIC, MINCED
- 1/2 CUP DRY WHITE WINE
- 2 TABLESPOONS OLIVE OIL
- 2 TABLESPOONS UNSALTED BUTTER
- 2 TABLESPOONS FRESH PARSLEY, CHOPPED
- SALT AND PEPPER TO TASTE
- LEMON WEDGES FOR GARNISH

INSTRUCTIONS

- HEAT THE OLIVE OIL IN A WIDE, SHALLOW PAN OVER MEDIUM HEAT. ADD THE CHOPPED ONIONS AND COOK UNTIL THEY BECOME TRANSLUCENT, ABOUT 2-3 MINUTES. STIR IN THE MINCED GARLIC AND COOK FOR AN ADDITIONAL MINUTE UNTIL FRAGRANT.
- ADD THE ARBORIO RICE TO THE PAN AND STIR TO COAT THE RICE WITH THE ONION AND GARLIC MIXTURE. COOK FOR ABOUT 2 MINUTES OR UNTIL THE RICE BECOMES SLIGHTLY TRANSLUCENT.
- POUR IN THE WHITE WINE AND COOK UNTIL IT IS MOSTLY ABSORBED BY THE RICE, STIRRING CONTINUOUSLY.
- BEGIN ADDING THE WARM CHICKEN OR VEGETABLE BROTH, ONE LADLEFUL AT A TIME, STIRRING FREQUENTLY. ALLOW THE LIQUID TO BE ABSORBED BY THE RICE BEFORE ADDING MORE. CONTINUE THIS PROCESS UNTIL THE RICE IS CREAMY AND COOKED AL DENTE, WHICH SHOULD TAKE ABOUT 18-20 MINUTES.
- WHILE THE RISOTTO IS COOKING, HEAT A SEPARATE PAN OVER MEDIUM-HIGH HEAT AND ADD A BIT OF OLIVE OIL. SEASON THE PRAWNS WITH SALT AND PEPPER, AND COOK THEM FOR ABOUT 2-3 MINUTES ON EACH SIDE OR UNTIL THEY TURN PINK AND OPAQUE. REMOVE THEM FROM THE PAN AND SET THEM ASIDE.
- WHEN THE RISOTTO IS READY, REMOVE IT FROM THE HEAT. STIR IN THE COOKED PRAWNS. SEASON WITH SALT AND PEPPER TO TASTE.
- FINISH THE DISH BY STIRRING IN THE BUTTER UNTIL IT MELTS AND MAKES THE RISOTTO EVEN CREAMIER. STIR IN FRESH CHOPPED PARSLEY
- SERVE THE PRAWN RISOTTO HOT, WITH LEMON WEDGES ON THE SIDE.

SPAGHETTI AGLIO E OLIO

SERVES: 4   PREP TIME: 5 MIN   TOTAL TIME: 20 MIN

INGREDIENTS

- 500G GOOD QUALITY SPAGHETTI
- 5 CLOVES GARLIC, THINLY SLICED
- 1/4 CUP EXTRA-VIRGIN OLIVE OIL
- 2 RED CHILLIES CHOPPED OR RED PEPPER FLAKES (TO TASTE)
- SALT AND BLACK PEPPER (TO TASTE)
- FRESH PARSLEY, CHOPPED

INSTRUCTIONS

- COOK THE SPAGHETTI ACCORDING TO PACKAGE INSTRUCTIONS. DRAIN AND SET ASIDE. <u>IF IT IS FRESH PASTA, THIS SHOULD ONLY BE COOKED FOR 3-4 MINUTES.</u>
- IN A PAN, HEAT THE OLIVE OIL OVER LOW HEAT. ADD GARLIC AND FRESH CHILLI OR CHILLI FLAKES. SAUTÉ UNTIL THE GARLIC TURNS GOLDEN BUT NOT BROWNED.
- TOSS THE COOKED SPAGHETTI INTO THE PAN AND COAT WITH THE GARLIC OIL.
- SEASON WITH SALT, BLACK PEPPER, AND FRESH PARSLEY. SERVE HOT.

ONE POT TOMATO BASIL PASTA

SERVES: 4   PREP TIME: 5 MIN   TOTAL TIME: 20 MIN

INGREDIENTS

- 300G SPAGHETTI OR ANY SHAPE PASTA
- 2 PUNNETS COLOURFUL CHERRY TOMATOES HALVED
- 3 CLOVES GARLIC, FINELY CHOPPED
- LOTS OF OLIVE OIL
- FRESH BASIL LEAVES
- PARMESAN
- SALT AND BLACK PEPPER (TO TASTE)

INSTRUCTIONS

- IN A LARGE POT, ADD DASH OLIVE OIL, FRY GARLIC THEN ADD HANDFUL OF BASIL AND HALVED TOMATOES AND COOK FOR 5-10 MINS.
- ADD 750ML OF HOT WATER, SALT & PEPPER, LEAVE TO BOIL.
- THEN ADD 500G OF DRIED SPAGHETTI
- LET ONE END SOFTEN, THEN STIR GENTLY FOR 10-12 MINS UNTIL IT THICKENS UP AND ALL OF THE SPAGHETTI HAS SOFTENED.
- PUT GENEROUS AMOUNT OF PARMESAN CHEESE AND STIR AGAIN
- THEN SERVE WITH BASIL ONCE PASTA IS AL DENTE.

RIGATONI ALL'AMATRICIANA

SERVES: 6   PREP TIME: 5 MIN   TOTAL TIME: 25 MIN

INGREDIENTS

- **500G OF PEELED WHOLE TOMATOES**
- **500G OF RIGATONI PASTA**
- **15 OF SLICES OF BACON OR PANCETTA**
- **400G OF PECORINO CHEESE, GRATED**
- **ROSEMARY**
- **WHITE WINE**
- **EXTRA-VIRGIN OLIVE OIL**
- **SALT**
- **PEPPER**

INSTRUCTIONS

- START BY BRINGING A LARGE POT OF SALTED WATER TO THE BOIL. COOK THE RIGATONI ACCORDING TO THE PACKAGE INSTRUCTIONS UNTIL AL DENTE. DRAIN AND SET ASIDE. *<u>IF IT IS FRESH PASTA, THIS SHOULD ONLY BE COOKED FOR 3-4 MINUTES.</u>
- IN A LARGE PAN, HEAT A DRIZZLE OF EXTRA-VIRGIN OLIVE OIL OVER MEDIUM HEAT. ADD THE DICED PANCETTA OR BACON AND COOK UNTIL IT BECOMES CRISPY AND THE FAT HAS RENDERED, ABOUT 4-5 MINUTES.
- ADD THE CHOPPED ONION TO THE PAN WITH THE PANCETTA AND SAUTÉ UNTIL THE ONION BECOMES SOFT AND TRANSLUCENT, ABOUT 2-3 MINUTES.
- IF USING WHITE WINE, POUR IT INTO THE PAN, AND LET IT SIMMER FOR A COUPLE OF MINUTES, ALLOWING THE ALCOHOL TO EVAPORATE.
- ADD THE CRUSHED TOMATOES TO THE PAN AND SEASON WITH RED PEPPER FLAKES, SALT, AND BLACK PEPPER. REDUCE THE HEAT TO LOW AND SIMMER THE SAUCE FOR ABOUT 15-20 MINUTES, STIRRING OCCASIONALLY.
- ONCE THE SAUCE IS READY, TASTE AND ADJUST THE SEASONING IF NEEDED. PECORINO IS SALTY, SO BE CAUTIOUS WITH THE SALT.
- TOSS THE COOKED RIGATONI INTO THE PAN WITH THE AMATRICIANA SAUCE. MIX EVERYTHING TOGETHER UNTIL THE PASTA IS COATED EVENLY WITH THE SAUCE.
- SERVE THE RIGATONI ALL'AMATRICIANA HOT, GARNISHED WITH A GENEROUS AMOUNT OF GRATED PECORINO ON TOP.

Linguine

LINGUINI SMOKED TROUT + DILL

SERVES: 4   PREP TIME: 5 MIN   TOTAL TIME: 20 MIN

INGREDIENTS

- 4 TBSP EXTRA VIRGIN OLIVE OIL
- 1 SHALLOT, FINELY CHOPPED
- ½ GLASS WHITE WINE
- 200G CHERRY TOMATOES, HALVED
- A HANDFUL OF DILL, ROUGHLY CHOPPED
- SALT AND FRESHLY GROUND BLACK PEPPER
- 350G LINGUINE
- 200G SMOKED TROUT, ROUGHLY CHOPPED

INSTRUCTIONS

- HEAT THE OIL IN A FRYING PAN, ADD THE SHALLOT ON A MEDIUM HEAT UNTIL SOFT. INCREASE THE HEAT, ADD THE WINE AND ALLOW TO EVAPORATE. STIR IN THE TOMATOES AND HALF OF THE DILL AND SEASON WITH SALT AND PEPPER. REDUCE THE HEAT TO LOW, COVER WITH A LID AND LEAVE TO GENTLY SIMMER FOR 10 MINUTES. ADD THE SMOKED TROUT TO THE SAUCE, STIR THROUGH AND CONTINUE TO COOK FOR A COUPLE OF MINUTES.

- MEANWHILE, COOK THE LINGUINE IN PLENTY OF LIGHTLY SALTED BOILING WATER UNTIL AL DENTE.
- *_IF IT IS FRESH PASTA, THIS SHOULD ONLY BE COOKED FOR 3-4 MINUTES._
- DRAIN THE PASTA, RESERVING A COUPLE OF TABLESPOONS OF THE COOKING WATER. STIR THE PASTA AND COOKING WATER INTO THE SAUCE AND MIX TOGETHER WELL. REMOVE FROM THE HEAT, SPRINKLE WITH THE REMAINING DILL AND SERVE IMMEDIATELY.

SPAGHETTI VONGOLE

SERVES: 4   PREP TIME: 5 MIN   TOTAL TIME: 25 MIN

INGREDIENTS

- 500G SPAGHETTI
- 200ML OLIVE OIL
- 1KG FRESH CLAMS IN SHELLS
- 2 SMALL RED CHILLIES SEEDED & SLICED
- 200ML WHITE WINE
- 6 FLOWERING ZUCCHINI SHAVED
- 1/2 BUNCH FLAT LEAF PARSLEY CHOPPED
- JUICE OF 1 LEMON
- SALT & PEPPER

INSTRUCTIONS

- BRING A SAUCEPAN OF SALTED WATER TO THE BOIL AND ADD SPAGHETTI, COOK UNTIL ALMOST AL DENTE.
- *IF IT IS FRESH PASTA, THIS SHOULD ONLY BE COOKED FOR 3-4 MINUTES._
- WHILE SPAGHETTI IS COOKING, HEAT OIL IN A HEAVY SAUCEPAN OVER HIGH HEAT AND ADD CLAMS, GARLIC & CHILLI.
- STIR FOR ONE MINUTE THEN ADD WINE, CLOSE LID AND COOK FOR 4 MINUTES.
- ADD ZUCCHINI AND COOK FOR FURTHER 2 MINUTES OR UNTIL CLAMS HAVE OPENED.
- REMOVE CLOSED CLAMS.
- STRAIN SPAGHETTI AND ADD TO CLAMS.
- STIR THROUGH PARSLEY AND LEMON JUICE. SEASON WITH SALT AND PEPPER
- SERVE WITH CRUSTY BREAD.

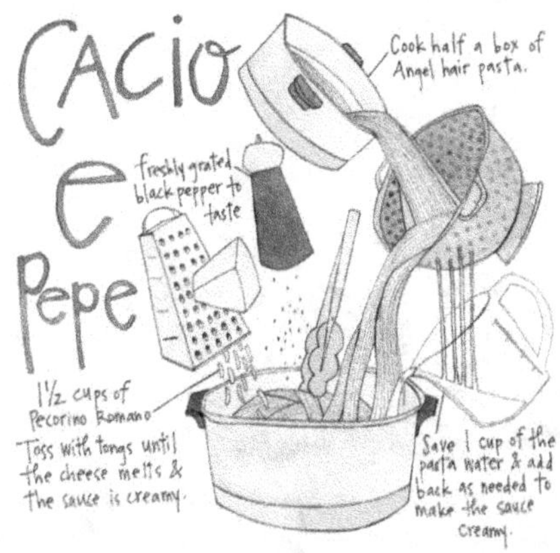

SPAGHETTI CACIO E PEPE

SERVES: 4   PREP TIME: 10 MIN   TOTAL TIME: 10 MIN

INGREDIENTS

- **400G HIGH QUALITY DRIED SPAGHETTI**
- **GRATED PECORINO ROMANO 240GR**
- **BLACK PEPPER**

INSTRUCTIONS

- BOIL SOME WATER IN A PAN (USE ABOUT HALF OF WHAT YOU USUALLY USE TO COOK PASTA, SO IT WILL BE RICHER IN STARCH) AND WHEN IT BOILS YOU CAN ADD SALT TO TASTE. ONCE SALTED, YOU CAN COOK THE SPAGHETTI.
- IN THE MEANTIME, POUR THE WHOLE PEPPERCORNS ON A CUTTING BOARD AND CRUSH THEM WITH A MORTAR & PESTLE OR A GRINDER, THIS WILL RELEASE MORE OF THE PUNGENT SCENT OF THE PEPPER.
- POUR HALF OF THE CRUSHED PEPPER INTO A LARGE NON-STICK PAN AND TOAST OVER LOW HEAT STIRRING WITH A WOODEN SPOON, THEN ADD A COUPLE OF LADLES OF COOKING WATER.
- THE BUBBLES YOU SEE APPEARING IN THE PASTA POT ARE FROM THE STARCH CONTAINED IN THE WATER. DRAIN THE SPAGHETTI WHEN IT IS VERY AL DENTE (KEEPING THE COOKING WATER ASIDE TO USE LATER) AND POUR THE PASTA DIRECTLY INTO THE PAN WITH TOASTED PEPPER, IT WILL CONTINUE COOKING WITH THE SEASONING.
- STIR THE PASTA CONTINUOUSLY WITH THE KITCHEN TONGS TO MAKE IT "BREATHE" & ADD LADLE OF WATER OR 2 IF NECESSARY, TO CONTINUE COOKING.
- KEEP POURING A LADLE OF WATER ONLY WHEN NEEDED (WHEN YOU SEE THAT THE PAN IS ALMOST COMPLETELY DRY) AND STIR WITH KITCHEN TONGS.
- THEN PREPARE THE PECORINO CREAM (DON'T START THIS EARLIER, THE CREAM WILL GET TOO THICK).
- FOR THE PECORINO CREAM, POUR ABOUT HALF OF THE GRATED PECORINO CHEESE INTO A BOWL. ADD A LADLE OF COOKING WATER TO THE GRATED PECORINO CHEESE AND STIR VIGOROUSLY WITH A WHISK, ADD MORE WATER WHEN NEEDED.
- THEN ADD THE REMAINING HALF OF THE PECORINO CHEESE, KEEPING A LITTLE BIT ASIDE TO GARNISH LATER. CHECK AND ADD A LITTLE MORE WATER IF NEEDED: AT THIS STAGE YOU WILL HAVE TO CAREFULLY ADJUST THE AMOUNT OF PECORINO CHEESE TO THE WATER TO OBTAIN A CREAM OF THE RIGHT CONSISTENCY AND WITHOUT LUMPS.
- FINISH COOKING YOUR PASTA, ADDING A LITTLE MORE HOT WATER IF NECESSARY, UNTIL IT'S AL DENTE, THEN BEFORE ADDING THE PECORINO CREAM, BRIEFLY STIR THE CREAM BY PLACING THE BOWL OVER THE STEAM OF THE PAN WITH HOT WATER, ALWAYS STIR WITH THE WHISK, YOU WANT TO BRING THE CREAM BACK TO A TEMPERATURE SIMILAR TO THE THAT OF YOUR PASTA.
- TURN THE HEAT OFF UNDER THE PAN WITH SPAGHETTI AND POUR IN THE PECORINO CREAM.
- WHILE POURING THE PECORINO CREAM ONTO YOUR SPAGHETTI, STIR IT CONTINUOUSLY WITH THE KITCHEN TONGS.THEN PUT THE PECORINO YOU KEPT ASIDE IN TOO AND STIR AND SAUTÉ THE PASTA AGAIN.
- TRANSFER YOUR SPAGHETTI CACIO E PEPE TO A PLATE AND SEASON WITH THE REMAINING PEPPER, ENJOY IMMEDIATELY IN ALL ITS CREAMINESS.

ORECCHIETTE WITH BROCCOLI + SALSICCIA

SERVES:4-6 PREP TIME: 10 MIN TOTAL TIME: 35 MIN

INGREDIENTS

- 500G ORECCHIETTE PASTA
- 450G ITALIAN SAUSAGE (SALSICCIA), EITHER MILD OR SPICY BASED ON YOUR PREFERENCE
- 1 LARGE HEAD OF BROCCOLI, CUT INTO SMALL FLORETS
- 2 CLOVES OF GARLIC, MINCED
- 1/4 CUP EXTRA-VIRGIN OLIVE OIL
- SALT AND PEPPER TO TASTE
- RED PEPPER FLAKES (OPTIONAL, FOR ADDED HEAT)
- GRATED PECORINO ROMANO OR PARMESAN CHEESE FOR SERVING

INSTRUCTIONS

- START BY BRINGING A LARGE POT OF SALTED WATER TO A BOIL. ONCE IT'S BOILING, ADD THE ORECCHIETTE PASTA AND COOK IT ACCORDING TO THE PACKAGE INSTRUCTIONS UNTIL IT'S AL DENTE. BEFORE DRAINING THE PASTA, RESERVE ABOUT 1/2 CUP OF THE COOKING WATER. DRAIN THE PASTA AND SET IT ASIDE. *IF IT IS FRESH PASTA, THIS SHOULD ONLY BE COOKED FOR 3-4 MINUTES.
- WHILE THE PASTA IS COOKING, REMOVE THE CASING FROM THE ITALIAN SAUSAGE AND CRUMBLE IT INTO A LARGE SKILLET OR PAN. COOK THE SAUSAGE OVER MEDIUM-HIGH HEAT, BREAKING IT APART WITH A SPOON, UNTIL IT'S BROWNED AND COOKED THROUGH. THIS SHOULD TAKE ABOUT 5-7 MINUTES. IF YOU'RE USING SPICY SAUSAGE, YOU CAN ADD RED PEPPER FLAKES FOR SOME HEAT.
- REMOVE THE COOKED SAUSAGE FROM THE PAN AND SET IT ASIDE. IN THE SAME PAN, ADD THE MINCED GARLIC AND COOK FOR ABOUT A MINUTE UNTIL IT BECOMES FRAGRANT.
- ADD THE BROCCOLI FLORETS TO THE PAN WITH THE GARLIC. SAUTE THEM FOR ABOUT 5-7 MINUTES OR UNTIL THEY BECOME TENDER AND SLIGHTLY BROWNED. IF THE PAN IS TOO DRY, YOU CAN ADD A BIT OF THE RESERVED PASTA COOKING WATER TO HELP STEAM THE BROCCOLI.
- ONCE THE BROCCOLI IS COOKED, RETURN THE COOKED SAUSAGE TO THE PAN AND MIX IT ALL TOGETHER.
- ADD THE COOKED ORECCHIETTE PASTA TO THE PAN WITH THE SAUSAGE AND BROCCOLI. DRIZZLE WITH THE EXTRA-VIRGIN OLIVE OIL AND TOSS EVERYTHING TOGETHER, MAKING SURE THE PASTA IS WELL COATED. IF THE MIXTURE SEEMS DRY, YOU CAN ADD MORE OF THE RESERVED PASTA COOKING WATER.
- SEASON THE DISH WITH SALT AND PEPPER TO TASTE. REMEMBER THAT THE SAUSAGE CAN BE QUITE FLAVORFUL, SO BE CAREFUL WITH THE SALT.
- SERVE THE ORECCHIETTE WITH BROCCOLI AND SALSICCIA HOT, GARNISHED WITH GRATED PECORINO ROMANO OR PARMESAN CHEESE. ENJOY

BAKED GNOCCHI WITH PUMPKIN

SERVES: 4   PREP TIME: 15 MIN   TOTAL TIME: 1 HOUR

INGREDIENTS

- 750G HIGH QUALITY, STORE-BOUGHT POTATO GNOCCHI
- 1/3 CUP OLIVE OIL
- 16 SAGE LEAVES
- 750G JAP PUMPKIN, CUT INTO 5MM-THICK SLICES
- 2 EGG YOLKS
- 600ML PURE CREAM
- 1/2 TSP FINELY GRATED NUTMEG
- 3/4 CUP GRATED MOZZARELLA
- 100G BLUE CHEESE, CRUMBLED
- ROASTED CHOPPED HAZELNUTS, TO SERVE

INSTRUCTIONS

- PREHEAT OVEN TO 200°C. GREASE A 32CM ROUND BAKING DISH.
- COOK GNOCCHI A FEW MINUTES LESS THAN PACKET INSTRUCTIONS, THEN DRAIN AND RINSE UNDER COLD WATER.
- *IF IT IS HOMEMADE GNOCCHI, THEN DO NOT COOK YET.
- TOSS PUMPKIN AND 1 TBS OIL IN A BOWL. COMBINE WITH GNOCCHI, EGG YOLKS, CREAM, NUTMEG, 1/2 CUP MOZZARELLA, HALF THE SAGE AND HALF THE BLUE CHEESE. SPOON INTO PREPARED DISH AND TOP WITH REMAINING 1/4 CUP (25G) MOZZARELLA.
- BAKE FOR 45-50 MINUTES OR UNTIL PUMPKIN IS TENDER.
- MEANWHILE, HEAT 1/4 CUP OLIVE OIL IN A FRYPAN OVER MEDIUM-HIGH HEAT. ADD THE REMAINING SAGE AND COOK. DRAIN ON PAPER TOWEL, RESERVE OIL.
- WHEN YOU BAKED GNOCCHI IS READY TO COME OUT OF THE OVEN TOP WITH NUTS, FRIED SAGE AND REMAINING 50G BLUE CHEESE.
- DRIZZLE WITH RESERVED SAGE OIL TO SERVE.

PIZZA DOUGH

SERVES: 4   PREP TIME: 15 MIN   TOTAL TIME: 45 MIN

INGREDIENTS

- 500G PIZZA FLOUR OR STRONG BAKERS FLOUR
- 1 TSP SALD
- 325ML WARM WATER
- 3 TSP DRY YEAST
- 60ML OLIVE OIL

INSTRUCTIONS

*THIS RECIPE WILL MAKE 2 LARGE PIZZAS AROUND 30-40CM

- IN A LARGE BOWL, SIFT FLOUR AND SALT TOGETHER AND MAKE A WELL IN THE CENTRE
- IN ANOTHER BOWL, WHISK WARM WATER, YEAST AND OIL TOGETHER THEN POUR IN THE FLOUR WELL.
- USE YOUR HANDS TO MIX THE INGREDIENTS INTO A WET, STICKY DOUGH.
- PUT THE DOUGH ONTO A FLOURED BENCH AND KNEAD FOR 10-15MINS ADDING MORE FLOUR IF NEEDED.
- REURN DOUGH TO A BOWL, COVER WITH A TEA TOWEL AND SET ASIDE IN A WARM PLACE, AWAY FROM ANY DRAFT, TO RISE FOR 1-2 HOURS OR UNTIL DOUGH HAS DOUBLED.
- AFTER THE DOUGH HAS RISEN, PUNCH IT DOWN TO RELEASE THE AIR BUBBLES. AT THIS POINT, YOU CAN DIVIDE THE DOUGH INTO SMALLER PORTIONS IF YOU WANT TO MAKE INDIVIDUAL PIZZAS.
- PREHEAT YOUR OVEN TO 475°F (245°C), OR AS HOT AS IT WILL GO.
- ROLL OUT THE DOUGH ON A LIGHTLY FLOURED SURFACE TO YOUR DESIRED THICKNESS. TRANSFER THE ROLLED-OUT DOUGH TO A BAKING SHEET OR PIZZA STONE THAT HAS BEEN LIGHTLY DUSTED WITH CORNMEAL, SEMOLINA OR FLOUR.

*SEE NEXT FEW PAGES FOR PIZZA TOPPING RECIPES

PROSCIUTTO + ROCKET PIZZA

SERVES: 4   PREP TIME: 45 MIN TOTAL TIME: 1 HOUR

INGREDIENTS

- SEE DOUGH RECIPEON PAGE 00
- 1 X 400G CAN OF PEELED TOMATOES
- 4 X GARLIC CLOVES
- 10 BASIL LEAVES
- SALT & PEPPER
- 400G FRESH MOZZARELLA TORN
- 20 THINLY SLICED PROSCIUTTO
- 2 GENEROUS HANDFULS OF ROCKET
- LEMON JUICE
- OLIVE OIL

INSTRUCTIONS

- AFTER YOU HAVE MADE THE DOUGH (PG 33), THE NEXT THING THAT NEEDS TO BE DONE IS THE TOMATO BASE:
- CHOP THE GARLIC AND ADD TO A PAN WITH OLIVE OIL AND A DASH OF DRIED OREGANO. THEN EMPTY THE CAN OF TOMATOES INTO THE PAN AND COOK ON A LOW HEAT FOR A MINIMUM OF 20-30MINS TO MAKE POMODORO SUGO.

THEN
- WAIT FOR THE SUGO TO COOL THEN SPREAD SAUCE EVENLY OVER DOUGH.
- ARRANGE BASIL LEAVES OVER THE TOMATO THEN LAY TORN MOZZARELLA AND SEASON.
- BAKE FOR 12-15 MINS OR UNTIL PIZZA BASE IS CRISPY THEN REMOVE FROM OVEN AND PLACE THIN LAYERS OF PROSCIUTTO OVER THE MOZZARELLA
- DRESS ROCKET WITH LEMON JUICE AND OLIVE OIL AND LAY OVER THE PROSCIUTTO BEFORE SERVING.

*THIS CAN BE MADE WITH SALAMI, SPECK OR HAM

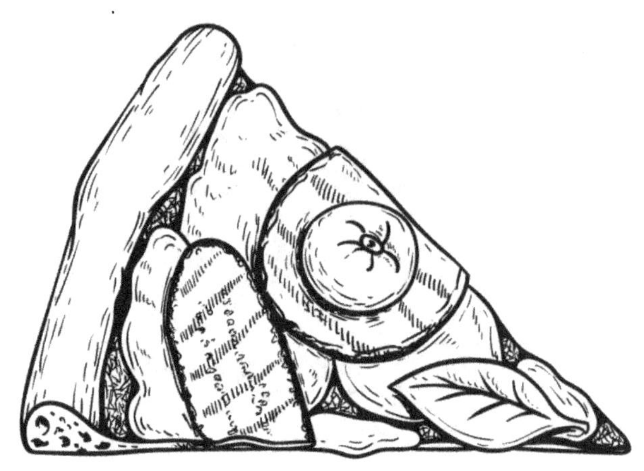

EGGPLANT + RICOTTA PIZZA

SERVES: 4   PREP TIME: 45 MIN TOTAL TIME: 1 HOUR

INGREDIENTS

- SEE DOUGH RECIPEON PAGE 00
- 1 X 400G CAN OF PEELED TOMATOES
- 4 X GARLIC CLOVES
- 10 BASIL LEAVES
- SALT & PEPPER
- 400G FRESH MOZZARELLA TORN
- 300G FRESH RICOTTA
- 2 MEDIUM EGGPLANTS SLICED INTO THIN DISCS

INSTRUCTIONS

- AFTER YOU HAVE MADE THE DOUGH (PG 33), THE NEXT THING THAT NEEDS TO BE DONE IS THE TOMATO BASE:
- CHOP THE GARLIC AND ADD TO A PAN WITH OLIVE OIL AND A DASH OF DRIED OREGANO. THEN EMPTY THE CAN OF TOMATOES INTO THE PAN AND COOK ON A LOW HEAT FOR A MINIMUM OF 20-30MINS TO MAKE POMODORO SUGO.

THEN
- LIGHTLY ROAST OR PAN FRY THE EGGPLANT DISCS AND SET ASIDE.
- ONCE THE SUGO HAS COOLED THEN SPREAD SAUCE EVENLY OVER DOUGH.
- ARRANGE BASIL LEAVES OVER THE TOMATO THEN LAY TORN MOZZARELLA AND SEASON.
- ADD LIGHTLY ROASTED EGGPLANT AND BLOB RICOTTA WITH A TEASPOON ALL OVER THE PIZZA.
- BAKE FOR 12-15 MINS OR UNTIL PIZZA BASE IS CRISPY THEN REMOVE FROM OVEN AND SERVE.

SECTION 4

SECONDO

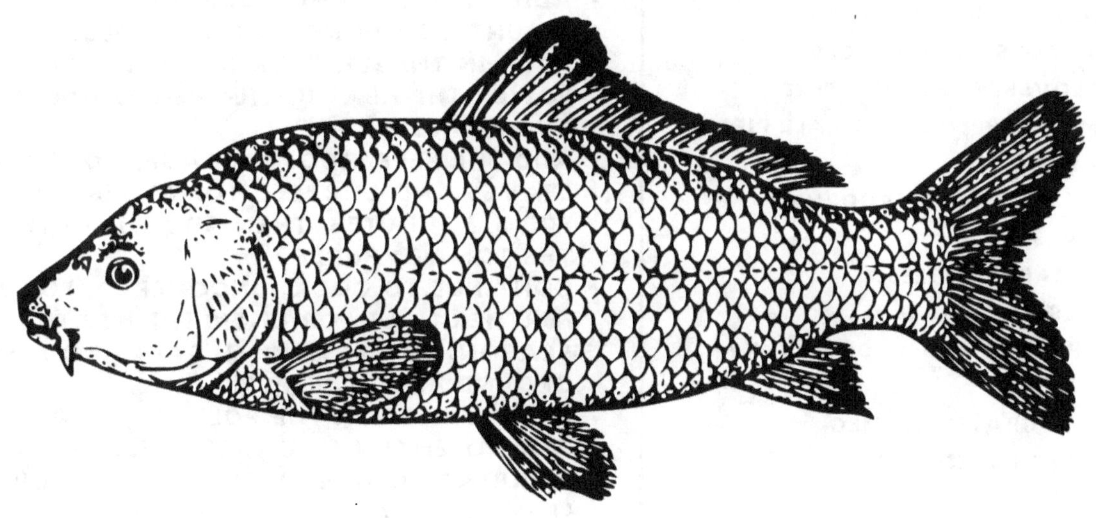

LAMB STEW WITH POLENTA

SERVES: 10   PREP TIME: 25 MIN   TOTAL TIME: 1.5 HRS

INGREDIENTS

FOR THE STEW
- 100ML OLIVE OIL
- 4 CELERY STALKS, FINELY DICED
- 1 LARGE ONION, FINELY CHOPPED
- 2 LARGE CARROTS, FINELY DICED
- 3 GARLIC CLOVES, FINELY CHOPPED
- 2.25KG LAMB CHOPPED INTO SMALL PIECES
- 200ML RED WINE
- 1 TSP WHOLE BLACK PEPPERCORNS
- 4 SAGE LEAVES
- 1 TBSP ROSEMARY NEEDLES
- 2 BAY LEAVES
- 1.5KG CHOPPED TOMATOES, OR CHUNKY PASSATA
- 1 TSP FRESHLY GRATED NUTMEG
- 2 TBSP TOMATO PURÉE
- SALT AND PEPPER

FOR THE POLENTA
- 4 TSP SALT
- 600G QUICK-COOK POLENTA
- 250G FONTINA CHEESE (OR TALEGGIO), FRESHLY GRATED
- 100G PARMESAN, FRESHLY GRATED
- 100G UNSALTED BUTTER

INSTRUCTIONS

- HEAT THE OIL IN A LARGE PAN AND FRY THE VEGETABLES AND GARLIC FOR 6-7 MINUTES, OR UNTIL SOFTENED.
- ADD THE MEAT AND COOK FOR 8-10 MINUTES, OR UNTIL BROWNED ON ALL SIDES.
- POUR IN THE WINE, BRING TO THE BOIL, THEN LOWER THE HEAT UNTIL THE MIXTURE IS SIMMERING.
- ADD THE PEPPERCORNS, SAGE, ROSEMARY, BAY LEAVES AND CHOPPED TOMATOES AND COOK FOR 5-6 MINUTES, THEN ADD THE NUTMEG AND THE TOMATO PURÉE.
- CONTINUE TO COOK, UNCOVERED, FOR A FURTHER HOUR, OR UNTIL THE MEAT IS TENDER. SEASON, TO TASTE WITH SALT AND FRESHLY GROUND BLACK PEPPER.
- MEANWHILE FOR THE POLENTA, COOK THE SALT AND POLENTA IN 3 LITRES BOILING WATER, STIRRING CONTINUOUSLY FOR 5-6 MINUTES (TAKE CARE AS THE MIXTURE MAY BUBBLE AND SPIT).
- REMOVE THE PAN FROM THE HEAT AND STIR IN THE CHEESES AND BUTTER. KEEP WARM.
- TO SERVE, SPREAD THE POLENTA ON TO A LARGE, CLEAN BOARD, MAKING A WELL IN THE MIDDLE, THEN POUR THE STEW INTO THE MIDDLE.
- PERFECT TO SHARE IN THE MIDDLE OF YOUR TABLE WITH FRIENDS

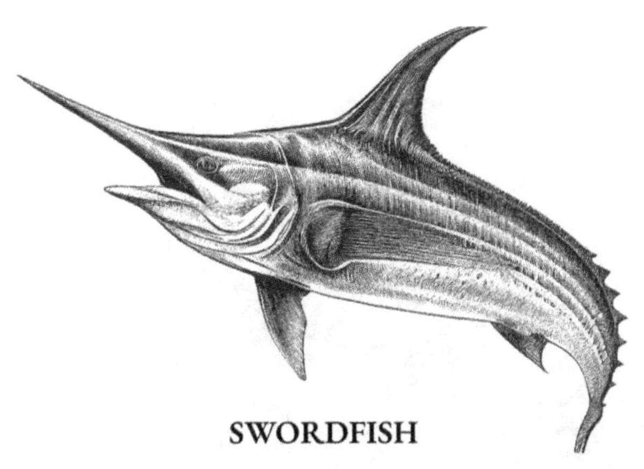

SWORDFISH

GRILLED SWORDFISH

SERVES: 4   PREP TIME: 15 MIN   TOTAL TIME: 45 MINS

INGREDIENTS

- 4 SWORDFISH STEAKS (ABOUT 6 OUNCES EACH)
- 1/4 CUP EXTRA VIRGIN OLIVE OIL
- 3 CLOVES GARLIC, MINCED
- 2 TABLESPOONS FRESH PARSLEY, CHOPPED
- 1 TABLESPOON FRESH LEMON JUICE
- 1 TEASPOON DRIED OREGANO
- SALT AND PEPPER TO TASTE
- LEMON WEDGES FOR SERVING
- VEGETABLES OF CHOICE (ROASTED SEPARATELY IN OVEN)

INSTRUCTIONS

- RINSE THE SWORDFISH STEAKS UNDER COLD WATER AND PAT THEM DRY WITH PAPER TOWELS.
- SEASON BOTH SIDES OF THE STEAKS WITH SALT AND PEPPER.

THE MARINADE:
- IN A SMALL BOWL, WHISK TOGETHER THE OLIVE OIL, MINCED GARLIC, CHOPPED PARSLEY, LEMON JUICE, AND DRIED OREGANO.
- PLACE THE SWORDFISH STEAKS IN A SHALLOW DISH. POUR THE MARINADE OVER THE STEAKS, ENSURING THEY ARE WELL-COATED.
- MARINATE THE SWORDFISH IN THE REFRIGERATOR FOR AT LEAST 30 MINUTES TO ALLOW THE FLAVORS TO INFUSE.
- PREHEAT YOUR GRILL TO MEDIUM-HIGH HEAT.
- REMOVE THE SWORDFISH FROM THE MARINADE AND LET ANY EXCESS DRIP OFF.
- PLACE THE STEAKS ON THE PREHEATED GRILL AND COOK FOR ABOUT 4-5 MINUTES PER SIDE. THE EXACT COOKING TIME MAY VARY BASED ON THE THICKNESS OF THE STEAKS.
- BASTE WITH MARINADE.
- ONCE THE SWORDFISH IS COOKED THROUGH, REMOVE FROM THE GRILL & DRIZZLE ANY REMAINING MARINADE OVER THE SWORDFISH.
- GARNISH WITH ADDITIONAL FRESH PARSLEY AND SERVE WITH LEMON WEDGES ON THE SIDE.
- DELICIOUS ON ITS OWN OR PAIRED WITH A SIDE OF ROASTED VEGETABLES.

SCALOPPINE AL LIMORE

SERVES: 4   PREP TIME: 15 MIN   TOTAL TIME: 40 MINS

INGREDIENTS

- 300-350GR VEAL SLICES (ABOUT 8-10 SLICES DEPENDING ON THE CUTTING)
- 1 LEMON ZEST AND 50ML JUICE
- 00 FLOUR FOR FLOURING
- 25G OF BUTTER
- EXTRA VIRGIN OLIVE OIL
- SALT UP TO TASTE
- PEPPER TO TASTE
- YOUR CHOICE OF LETTUCE

INSTRUCTIONS

- GRATE LEMON ZEST IN A LITTLE DISH. THEN SQUEEZE THE LEMON TO GET THE JUICE, ABOUT 50ML.

- BEAT THE SLICES OF VEAL WITH THE HELP OF A MEAT MALLET. COVER THEM WITH BAKING PAPER SO AS NOT TO BREAK THE FIBERS. HIT THEM WITH A FIRM HAND BUT WITHOUT REARING THE PULP.

- FLOUR THE VEAL SLICES; PREPARE A LARGE PAN, MELT A KNOB OF BUTTER WITH A DRIZZLE OF EXTRA VIRGIN OLIVE OIL IN A PAN OVER A LOW HEAT, THEN ADD THE SLICES, RAISE TO MEDIUM HEAT AND BROWN THE VEAL FOR A COUPLE OF MINUTES EACH SIDE.

- SEASON WITH SALT AND BLACK PEPPER, POUR THE LEMON JUICE INTO THE PAN AND COOK OVER LOW HEAT FOR 2-3MIN. AS SOON AS THE SAUCE BEGINS TO THICKEN, YOU CAN TURN OFF.

- SERVE RIGHT AWAY WITH THE CREAM THAT FORMED DURING COOKING AND WITH A DUST OF LEMON ZEST ON THE TOP.

- SERVE WITH LETTUCE DRIZZLED IN OLIVE OIL AND VINEGAR.

POLLO AL LIMONE, OLIVE, CAPPERI

SERVES: 4   PREP TIME: 15 MIN   TOTAL TIME: 45 MINS

INGREDIENTS

- 2 LEMONS, SLICED 1/4-INCH THICK
- 1/4 CUP EXTRA-VIRGIN OLIVE OIL
- SALT AND FRESHLY GROUND LEMON PEPPER
- 4-5 LARGE CHICKEN BREASTS, SKINLESS, BONELESS
- ALL-PURPOSE FLOUR, FOR DUSTING
- 2 TABLESPOONS CAPERS, DRAINED, RINSED
- 1/2 CUP CASTELVETRANA OLIVES, PITTED, SLICED
- 1 CUP CHICKEN STOCK
- 3 TABLESPOONS BUTTER, UNSALTED, CUT INTO SMALL PIECES
- 2 TABLESPOONS ITALIAN PARSLEY, CHOPPED
- 4 HANDFULS OF ROCKET

INSTRUCTIONS

- PLACE THE LEMONS ON A PARCHMENT-LINED BAKING SHEET IN A SINGLE LAYER. LIGHTLY DRIZZLE THE SLICES WITH OLIVE OIL AND SEASON WITH SALT AND PEPPER. ROAST IN A 180°C OVEN FOR 20 MINUTES, EDGES WILL BEGIN TO BROWN.

- SEASON THE CHICKEN WITH SALT AND PEPPER AND DUST THEM WITH FLOUR. SHAKE OF EXCESS FLOUR. USING A DEEP SKILLET, HEAT THE OIL AND COOK CHICKEN ON MEDIUM-HIGH HEAT UNTIL GOLDEN BROWN ON BOTH SIDES.

- ADD THE CAPERS, OLIVES AND STOCK, BRING TO A BOIL. COOK OVER MEDIUM HEAT UNTIL THE STOCK IS REDUCED, ABOUT 5 MINUTES.

- STIR IN THE BUTTER UNTIL MELTED. ADD THE ROASTED LEMONS AND PARSLEY. TASTE SAUCE FOR SEASONING AND IF NECESSARY, ADD SALT AND PEPPER. SIMMER UNTIL CHICKEN IS COMPLETELY COOKED.

- TO SERVE, PLACE ROCKET IN INDIVIDUAL BOWLS OR A LARGE PLATTER FOR FAMILY STYLE. PLACE THE CHICKEN (SLICED EACH BREAST) ON TOP OF THE ROCKET AND GENEROUSLY SPOON THE SAUCE OVER THE ENTIRE DISH.

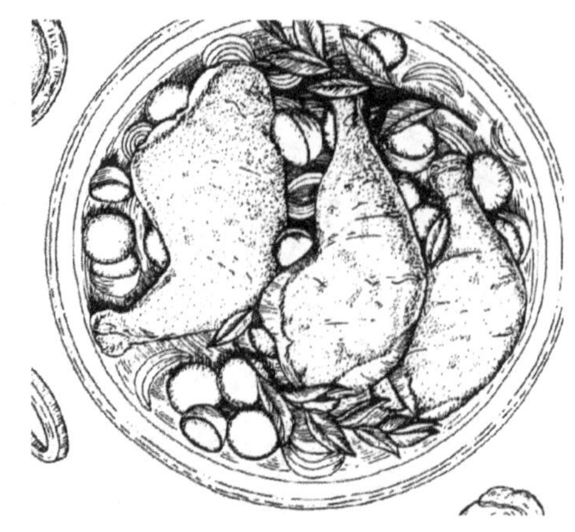

POLLO ALLA CACCIATORA

SERVES: 4 PREP TIME: 10 MIN TOTAL TIME: 40 MINS

INGREDIENTS

- 4-6 CHICKEN THIGHS
- 1/2 CUP ALL-PURPOSE FLOUR
- SALT AND PEPPER TO TASTE
- 3 TABLESPOONS OLIVE OIL
- 1 ONION, SLICED
- 2 CLOVES GARLIC, MINCED
- 1 BELL PEPPER, SLICED
- 1 CUP MUSHROOMS, SLICED
- 1 CUP RED WINE
- 1 CAN (28 OZ) CRUSHED TOMATOES
- 1 TEASPOON DRIED OREGANO
- 1 TEASPOON DRIED BASIL
- 1/2 TEASPOON RED PEPPER FLAKES
  (OPTIONAL)

INSTRUCTIONS

- LADLE CHICKEN IN FLOUR, SALT, AND
  PEPPER. BROWN IN SKILLET WITH OLIVE OIL.

- SAUTÉ ONION, GARLIC, BELL PEPPER, AND
  MUSHROOMS UNTIL SOFTENED IN ANOTHER
  PAN.

- POUR IN WINE, ADD TOMATOES, OREGANO,
  BASIL, AND RED PEPPER FLAKES. SIMMER.

- ADD CHICKEN BACK TO THE PAN, COVER,
  AND SIMMER UNTIL CHICKEN IS COOKED.

OSSO BUCO

SERVES: 4   PREP TIME: 15 MIN   TOTAL TIME: 2.5 HRS

INGREDIENTS

- 4-6 VEAL SHANKS
- 1 CUP FLOUR
- SALT AND PEPPER TO TASTE
- 2 TABLESPOONS OLIVE OIL
- 1 ONION, FINELY CHOPPED
- 2 CARROTS, DICED
- 2 CELERY STALKS, DICED
- 3 CLOVES GARLIC, MINCED
- 1 CUP DRY WHITE WINE
- 1 CAN (14 OZ) CRUSHED TOMATOES
- 1 CUP BEEF BROTH
- 2 BAY LEAVES
- 1 TEASPOON DRIED THYME

INSTRUCTIONS

- SEASON VEAL SHANKS WITH SALT AND PEPPER, THEN DREDGE IN FLOUR.

- IN A LARGE SKILLET, HEAT OLIVE OIL OVER MEDIUM-HIGH HEAT. BROWN VEAL SHANKS ON ALL SIDES AND SET ASIDE.

- IN THE SAME SKILLET, SAUTÉ ONION, CARROTS, CELERY, AND GARLIC UNTIL SOFTENED.

- POUR IN WHITE WINE, SCRAPING UP ANY BROWNED BITS. ADD TOMATOES, BEEF BROTH, BAY LEAVES AND THYME.

- RETURN VEAL SHANKS TO THE SKILLET, COVER, AND SIMMER FOR 2-3 HOURS OR UNTIL MEAT IS TENDER.

SALTIMBOCCA ALLA ROMANA

SERVES: 4   PREP TIME: 10 MIN   TOTAL TIME: 45 MINS

INGREDIENTS

- 4-6 VEAL CUTLETS
- 4-6 SLICES PROSCIUTTO
- 4-6 FRESH SAGE LEAVES
- FLOUR FOR DREDGING
- SALT AND PEPPER TO TASTE
- 2 TABLESPOONS OLIVE OIL
- 1/2 CUP DRY WHITE WINE
- 1/2 CUP CHICKEN BROTH
- 2 TABLESPOONS BUTTER

INSTRUCTIONS

- PLACE A SAGE LEAF ON EACH VEAL CUTLET, THEN WRAP WITH A SLICE OF PROSCIUTTO AND SECURE WITH TOOTHPICKS.

- COAT THE VEAL IN FLOUR, SEASONED WITH SALT AND PEPPER.

- IN A SKILLET, HEAT OLIVE OIL OVER MEDIUM-HIGH HEAT. COOK VEAL UNTIL BROWNED ON BOTH SIDES.

- REMOVE VEAL FROM THE SKILLET. POUR IN WHITE WINE AND CHICKEN BROTH, SCRAPING UP ANY BROWNED BITS.

- RETURN VEAL TO THE SKILLET, SIMMER FOR A FEW MINUTES. SWIRL IN BUTTER BEFORE SERVING.

MELANZANE ALLA PARMIGIANA

SERVES: 4 PREP TIME: 30 MIN TOTAL TIME: 1 HR

INGREDIENTS

- 2 LARGE EGGPLANTS, SLICED EVENLY ABOUT 1/2 CM THICK
- SALT
- 2 CUPS TOMATO SAUCE
- 1 CUP GRATED PARMESAN CHEESE
- 1 CUP MOZZARELLA CHEESE, SHREDDED
- FRESH BASIL LEAVES
- OLIVE OIL FOR FRYING

INSTRUCTIONS

- SALT EGGPLANT SLICES AND LET THEM SIT FOR 30 MINUTES. PAT DRY WITH PAPER TOWELS.

- HEAT OLIVE OIL IN A PAN AND FRY EGGPLANT SLICES UNTIL GOLDEN BROWN.

- PREHEAT OVEN TO 375°F (190°C).

- IN A BAKING DISH, LAYER FRIED EGGPLANT, TOMATO SAUCE, PARMESAN, AND MOZZARELLA. REPEAT.

- TOP WITH FRESH BASIL LEAVES. BAKE FOR 25-30 MINUTES OR UNTIL BUBBLY AND GOLDEN.

PORCHETTA

SERVES: 4   PREP TIME: 30 MIN TOTAL TIME: 1 HR

INGREDIENTS

- 1 WHOLE PORK BELLY
  (ABOUT 2-2.25 KG)
- 1 TABLESPOON FENNEL SEEDS
- 2 TABLESPOONS ROSEMARY,
  CHOPPED
- 4 CLOVES GARLIC, MINCED
- ZEST OF 1 LEMON
- SALT AND BLACK PEPPER TO TASTE
- OLIVE OIL

INSTRUCTIONS

- PREHEAT YOUR OVEN TO 325°F (160-170°C).

- SCORE THE PORK BELLY SKIN IN A CRISSCROSS PATTERN

- IN A MORTAR AND PESTLE, CRUSH THE FENNEL SEEDS AND
  MIX THEM WITH ROSEMARY, MINCED GARLIC, LEMON
  ZEST, SALT AND PEPPER.

- RUB THE PORK BELLY WITH OLIVE OIL AND THEN
  GENEROUSLY COAT IT WITH THE HERB MIXTURE, MAKING
  SURE TO GET IT INTO THE SCORED SKIN.

- ROLL UP THE PORK BELLY AND TIE IT SECURELY WITH
  KITCHEN TWINE.

- PLACE THE PORCHETTA ON A ROASTING PAN AND ROAST
  IN THE PREHEATED OVEN FOR ABOUT 3 HOURS OR UNTIL
  THE INTERNAL TEMPERATURE REACHES 160°F (71°C).

- CHECK THE SKIN/CRACKLING, IF IT IS NOT CRISPY YOU
  MAY NEED TO CHANGE THE OVEN TO GRILL FOR A FEW
  MINUTES - BUT KEEP AN EYE ON IT.

- ALLOW IT TO REST FOR 15 MINUTES BEFORE SLICING.
  SERVE THE PORCHETTA SLICES WITH YOUR FAVORITE
  SIDE DISHES OR INSIDE A SANDWICH WITH ROCKET AND
  AIOLI.

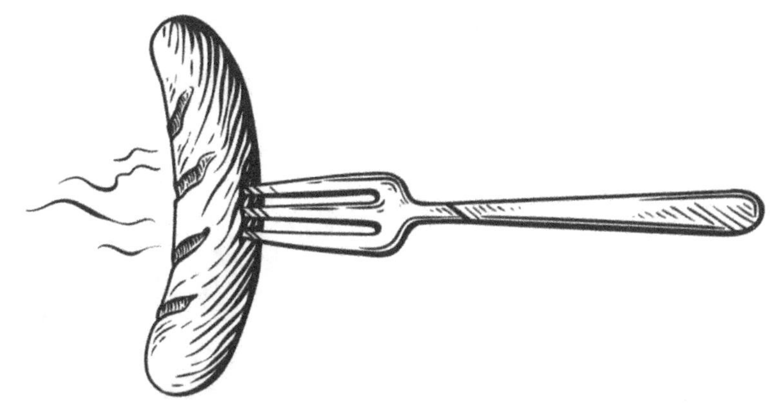

GRILLED ITALIAN SALSICCIA

SERVES: 4   PREP TIME: 10 MIN   TOTAL TIME: 1 HR

INGREDIENTS

- 500G-1KG FENNEL OR HOT ITALIAN SAUSAGES
- 2 TABLESPOONS OLIVE OIL
- 1 ONION, THINLY SLICED
- 2 BELL PEPPERS (RED AND GREEN), SLICED
- 3 CLOVES GARLIC, MINCED
- SALT AND BLACK PEPPER TO TASTE
- 1 TEASPOON DRIED OREGANO
- 1 TEASPOON DRIED BASIL
- 1/2 TEASPOON RED PEPPER FLAKES (OPTIONAL)
- 1/2 CUP (120ML) RED WINE (OPTIONAL)
- FRESH PARSLEY, CHOPPED (FOR GARNISH)
- ROLLS OR BREAD FOR SERVING

INSTRUCTIONS

- PREHEAT YOUR GRILL TO MEDIUM-HIGH HEAT THEN PRICK THE SAUSAGES WITH A FORK IN A FEW PLACES. THIS HELPS THEM COOK EVENLY AND ALLOWS EXCESS FAT TO ESCAPE.

- PLACE THE SAUSAGES ON THE PREHEATED GRILL, TURNING OCCASIONALLY, UNTIL THEY ARE COOKED THROUGH AND HAVE A NICE CHAR, USUALLY ABOUT 15-20 MINUTES.

- WHILE THE SAUSAGES ARE GRILLING, HEAT OLIVE OIL IN A LARGE SKILLET OVER MEDIUM HEAT. ADD SLICED ONIONS, BELL PEPPERS, AND MINCED GARLIC. SAUTÉ UNTIL THE VEGETABLES ARE SOFTENED AND SLIGHTLY CARAMELIZED.

- SEASON THE SAUTÉED VEGETABLES WITH SALT, BLACK PEPPER, DRIED OREGANO, DRIED BASIL, RED PEPPER FLAKES IF YOU WANT A BIT OF HEAT.

DEGLAZE WITH WINE (OPTIONAL):
- POUR WINE INTO THE SKILLET TO DEGLAZE, SCRAPE ANY BROWNED BITS FROM BOTTOM OF THE PAN. ALLOW WINE TO COOK DOWN FOR A FEW MINUTES

- ADD THE GRILLED SAUSAGES TO THE SKILLET WITH THE SAUTÉED VEGETABLES. TOSS EVERYTHING TOGETHER TO COAT THE SAUSAGES IN THE FLAVORFUL MIXTURE.

- SPOON THE SAUSAGE AND VEGETABLE MIXTURE INTO BREAD ROLLS OR ONTO A PLATE. GARNISH WITH FRESH CHOPPED PARSLEY.

SECTION 5

DOLCI

CLASSIC TIRAMISU

SERVES:4-6 PREP TIME: 30 MIN TOTAL TIME: 4 HRS

INGREDIENTS

- 6 EGG YOLKS
- 3/4 CUP GRANULATED SUGAR
- 1 CUP MASCARPONE CHEESE
- 1 1/2 CUPS HEAVY CREAM
- 2 CUPS BREWED ESPRESSO, COOLED TO ROOM TEMPERATURE
- 1/3 CUP COFFEE LIQUEUR (SUCH AS KAHLUA) OR DARK RUM
- 2 PACKS (ABOUT 7 OUNCES EACH) LADYFINGER COOKIES (SAVOIARDI)
- COCOA POWDER, FOR DUSTING

INSTRUCTIONS

- IN A LARGE BOWL, WHISK TOGETHER THE EGG YOLKS AND SUGAR UNTIL WELL COMBINED AND PALE YELLOW.
- ADD THE MASCARPONE CHEESE TO THE EGG YOLK MIXTURE AND WHISK UNTIL SMOOTH AND CREAMY.
- IN A SEPARATE BOWL, WHIP THE HEAVY CREAM UNTIL STIFF PEAKS FORM. GENTLY FOLD THE WHIPPED CREAM INTO THE MASCARPONE MIXTURE UNTIL FULLY INCORPORATED. SET ASIDE.
- IN A SHALLOW DISH, COMBINE THE BREWED ESPRESSO AND COFFEE LIQUEUR (OR RUM). DIP EACH LADYFINGER COOKIE INTO THE ESPRESSO MIXTURE FOR ABOUT 1-2 SECONDS, MAKING SURE NOT TO SOAK THEM TOO MUCH.
- ARRANGE A LAYER OF SOAKED LADYFINGER COOKIES IN THE BOTTOM OF A 9X13 INCH DISH, BREAKING THEM IF NECESSARY TO FIT.
- SPREAD HALF OF THE MASCARPONE MIXTURE OVER THE LAYER OF LADYFINGERS, SMOOTHING IT OUT WITH A SPATULA.
- REPEAT THE PROCESS WITH ANOTHER LAYER OF SOAKED LADYFINGER COOKIES AND THE REMAINING MASCARPONE MIXTURE.
- COVER THE DISH WITH PLASTIC WRAP AND REFRIGERATE FOR AT LEAST 4 HOURS, OR PREFERABLY OVERNIGHT, TO ALLOW THE FLAVORS TO MELD AND THE TIRAMISU TO SET.
- BEFORE SERVING, DUST THE TOP OF THE TIRAMISU WITH COCOA POWDER USING A FINE-MESH SIEVE.
- SLICE AND SERVE CHILLED. ENJOY YOUR DELICIOUS HOMEMADE TIRAMISU!
- NOTE: TIRAMISU IS BEST WHEN ALLOWED TO CHILL IN THE REFRIGERATOR FOR SEVERAL HOURS OR OVERNIGHT BEFORE SERVING, AS THIS ALLOWS THE FLAVORS TO DEVELOP AND THE TEXTURE TO SET PROPERLY.

VANILLA PANNA COTTA

SERVES: 4-6 PREP TIME: 30 MIN TOTAL TIME: 4 HRS

INGREDIENTS

- 2 CUPS HEAVY CREAM
- 1/2 CUP WHOLE MILK
- 1/2 CUP GRANULATED SUGAR
- 1 VANILLA BEAN POD (OR 2 TEASPOONS VANILLA EXTRACT)
- 2 1/4 TEASPOONS POWDERED GELATIN
- 3 TABLESPOONS COLD WATER
- OPTIONAL: FRESH BERRIES OR CHOPPED MANGO

INSTRUCTIONS

- POUR THE MILK INTO A SMALL BOWL. SPRINKLE THE POWDERED GELATIN OVER THE MILK AND LET IT SIT FOR ABOUT 5-10 MINUTES TO BLOOM.
- IN A SAUCEPAN, COMBINE THE HEAVY CREAM AND GRANULATED SUGAR. IF YOU'RE USING A VANILLA BEAN POD, SPLIT IT OPEN LENGTHWISE AND SCRAPE OUT THE SEEDS. ADD BOTH THE SEEDS AND THE POD TO THE CREAM MIXTURE. IF USING VANILLA EXTRACT, YOU'LL ADD IT LATER.
- HEAT THE CREAM MIXTURE OVER MEDIUM HEAT, STIRRING OCCASIONALLY, UNTIL IT JUST STARTS TO SIMMER. REMOVE IT FROM THE HEAT.
- IF YOU USED A VANILLA BEAN POD, REMOVE IT FROM THE CREAM MIXTURE. IF YOU'RE USING VANILLA EXTRACT, STIR IT INTO THE CREAM MIXTURE NOW.
- ADD THE BLOOMED GELATIN MIXTURE TO THE HOT CREAM MIXTURE, STIRRING UNTIL THE GELATIN IS COMPLETELY DISSOLVED.
- DIVIDE THE MIXTURE AMONG YOUR SERVING GLASSES OR MOLDS. YOU CAN USE SMALL RAMEKINS, GLASSES, OR SILICONE MOLDS, DEPENDING ON YOUR PREFERENCE.
- ALLOW THE PANNA COTTA TO COOL TO ROOM TEMPERATURE, THEN COVER EACH ONE WITH PLASTIC WRAP AND REFRIGERATE FOR AT LEAST 4 HOURS, OR UNTIL SET.
- ONCE SET, YOU CAN SERVE THE PANNA COTTA DIRECTLY IN THE GLASSES OR UNMOLD THEM ONTO SERVING PLATES. TO UNMOLD, DIP THE BOTTOM OF EACH MOLD INTO HOT WATER FOR A FEW SECONDS, THEN RUN A KNIFE AROUND THE EDGE TO LOOSEN THE PANNA COTTA. INVERT ONTO A PLATE AND GENTLY TAP TO RELEASE.
- SERVE THE PANNA COTTA CHILLED, WITH FRESH BERRIES, FRUIT COULIS, OR A SPRINKLE OF POWDERED SUGAR IF DESIRED.

RASBERRY RICOTTA CUP

SERVES:6   PREP TIME: 20 MIN   TOTAL TIME: 20 MINS

INGREDIENTS

- 1 CUP RICOTTA CHEESE
- 3 TBSP. SUGAR
- 2 TSP. FRESHLY GRATED ORANGE PEEL
- 1/2 TSP. VANILLA EXTRACT
- 1 CUP HEAVY (WHIPPING) CREAM
- 1 PUNNET RASPBERRIES
- 1/4 CUP FRESH ORANGE JUICE
- GARNISH: TOASTED SLICED ALMONDS

INSTRUCTIONS

- HAVE READY 6 DESSERT GLASSES.

- PROCESS RICOTTA, SUGAR, GRATED ORANGE PEEL AND VANILLA EXTRACT IN BLENDER OR FOOD PROCESSOR UNTIL SMOOTH

- BEAT CREAM UNTIL STIFF. FOLD IN RICOTTA MIXTURE.

- GENTLY TOSS RASPBERRIES WITH ORANGE JUICE TO MOISTEN.

- SPOON HALF THE RICOTTA CREAM INTO A LARGE STURDY ZIPTOP BAG OR SOME FOLDED BAKING PAPER (REFILLING WHEN NECESSARY). CUT A SMALL OPENING OFF 1 CORNER OF BAG.

- START THE LAYERING PROCESS: PUT 3 OR 4 RASPBERRIES IN BOTTOM OF EACH GLASS. PIPE ON ABOUT 1/2 THE RICOTTA CREAM. TOP WITH REMAINING BERRIES, THEN REMAINING RICOTTA CREAM. GARNISH WITH ALMONDS.

BLOOD ORANGE FINISHER

SERVES: 4-6 PREP TIME: 10 MIN TOTAL TIME: 20 MIN

INGREDIENTS

- 1/2 CUP CASTER SUGAR
- 1 1/2 CUPS FILTERED WATER
- 2 CARDAMON PODS (SQUASHED)
- 1 CINNAMON STICK
- 25MM BRUISED GINGER (SLIGHTLY SQUASHED)
- 4 BLOOD ORANGES
- 3 ORANGES

INSTRUCTIONS

- PUT ALL OF THE INGREDIENTS EXCLUDING THE ORANGES IN A PAN AND SIMMER FOR 5 MINUTES.

- WHILE YOU WAIT CAREFULLY PEEL THE ORANGES AND THINLY SLICE THEM WHOLE SO THEY COME OUT ROUND WITH NO RIND.

- GO BACK TO YOUR PAN, TURN OFF THE HEAT THEN LET IT COOL.

- ONCE COOLED STRAIN INTO A SERVING BOWL.

- ADD THE SLICED ORANGES.

- PUT IT IN THE FRIDGE FOR AN HOUR TO COOL.

- SERVE IN INDIVIDUAL BOWLS.

- YES, IT IS LIKE A DESSERT SOUP.

AFFOGATO

SERVES:4+   PREP TIME: 10 MIN TOTAL TIME: 20 MIN

INGREDIENTS PER SERVE

- 1 SHOT OF HOT ESPRESSO (YOU CAN ADJUST THE STRENGTH TO YOUR PREFERENCE)
- 1 SCOOP OF HIGH-QUALITY VANILLA GELATO OR ICE CREAM
- OPTIONAL: COCOA POWDER, CHOCOLATE SHAVINGS
- OPTIONAL: AMARETTO. FRANGELICO.

INSTRUCTIONS

- BREW A SHOT OF ESPRESSO USING YOUR PREFERRED METHOD (ESPRESSO MACHINE, STOVETOP ESPRESSO MAKER, OR COFFEE MAKER).
- WHILE THE ESPRESSO IS BREWING, PLACE A SCOOP OF VANILLA GELATO OR ICE CREAM INTO A HEAT-RESISTANT GLASS OR CUP.
- ONCE THE ESPRESSO IS READY, POUR IT DIRECTLY OVER THE GELATO.
- ALLOW THE ESPRESSO TO MELT THE GELATO SLIGHTLY, CREATING A CREAMY TEXTURE.
- IF DESIRED, SPRINKLE COCOA POWDER OR CHOCOLATE SHAVINGS OVER THE TOP FOR EXTRA FLAVOR AND PRESENTATION.
- OPTIONALLY, YOU CAN ADD A SPLASH OF LIQUEUR SUCH AS AMARETTO OR FRANGELICO FOR ADDITIONAL DEPTH OF FLAVOR.
- SERVE IMMEDIATELY AND ENJOY YOUR HOMEMADE AFFOGATO!

NOTE: THE KEY TO A GREAT AFFOGATO IS USING HIGH-QUALITY INGREDIENTS, ESPECIALLY GOOD-QUALITY ESPRESSO AND CREAMY GELATO OR ICE CREAM. YOU CAN ALSO EXPERIMENT WITH DIFFERENT FLAVORS OF GELATO OR ICE CREAM TO CREATE UNIQUE VARIATIONS OF THIS CLASSIC DESSERT.

BISCOTTI

INGREDIENTS

- 2 CUPS (250G) ALL-PURPOSE FLOUR OR ALMOND FLOUR
- 1 CUP (200G) GRANULATED SUGAR
- 1 TEASPOON BAKING POWDER
- 1/4 TEASPOON SALT
- 3 LARGE EGGS
- 1 TEASPOON VANILLA EXTRACT
- 1 CUP (150G) WHOLE ALMONDS, TOASTED AND COARSELY CHOPPED

INSTRUCTIONS

- PREHEAT OVEN TO 350°F (175°C). LINE A BAKING SHEET WITH PARCHMENT PAPER OR SILICONE BAKING MAT.
- IN A LARGE MIXING BOWL, COMBINE THE FLOUR, SUGAR, BAKING POWDER AND SALT.
- IN A SEPARATE BOWL, BEAT THE EGGS AND VANILLA EXTRACT TOGETHER. POUR THE EGG MIXTURE INTO THE DRY INGREDIENTS AND MIX UNTIL A DOUGH FORMS.
- FOLD IN THE CHOPPED ALMONDS INTO THE DOUGH UNTIL EVENLY DISTRIBUTED.
- TRANSFER THE DOUGH ONTO A FLOURED SURFACE AND DIVIDE IT INTO TWO EQUAL PORTIONS. SHAPE EACH PORTION INTO A LOG ABOUT 12 INCHES LONG AND 2 INCHES WIDE. PLACE THE LOGS ONTO THE PREPARED BAKING SHEET, LEAVING SPACE BETWEEN THEM AS THEY WILL SPREAD DURING BAKING.
- <u>FIRST BAKE</u>: BAKE THE LOGS IN THE PREHEATED OVEN FOR ABOUT 25-30 MINUTES, OR UNTIL THEY ARE FIRM AND LIGHTLY GOLDEN BROWN. REMOVE FROM THE OVEN AND LET THEM COOL FOR ABOUT 10-15 MINUTES.
- SLICE BISCOTTI USING A SERRATED KNIFE, SLICE THE LOGS DIAGONALLY INTO 1/2 INCH THICK SLICES. PLACE THE SLICES CUT SIDE DOWN ON THE BAKING SHEET.
- <u>SECOND BAKE</u>: RETURN THE BISCOTTI TO THE OVEN AND BAKE FOR AN ADDITIONAL 10-15 MINUTES, OR UNTIL THEY ARE CRISP AND GOLDEN BROWN.
- COOL: ONCE BAKED, REMOVE FROM THE OVEN AND LET THEM COOL COMPLETELY ON A WIRE RACK.

- SERVE THE BISCOTTI WITH COFFEE, TEA, OR AS A DESSERT. STORE IN AN AIRTIGHT CONTAINER AT ROOM TEMPERATURE FOR UP TO TWO WEEKS.

CONCLUSION

IN CONCLUSION, THIS ITALIAN COOKBOOK IS NOT MERELY A COLLECTION OF RECIPES; IT IS A CELEBRATION OF THE RICH CULINARY HERITAGE AND VIBRANT FLAVORS OF ITALY. FROM NORTHERN TO SOUTHERN ITALY, EACH DISH EMBODIES THE PASSION, TRADITION, AND ARTISTRY OF ITALIAN COOKING.

THROUGH THESE PAGES, WE HAVE EMBARKED ON A JOURNEY, EXPLORING THE DIVERSE REGIONS AND INGREDIENTS THAT MAKE ITALIAN CUISINE SO BELOVED AROUND THE WORLD. WE'VE LEARNED THE IMPORTANCE OF SIMPLICITY, QUALITY INGREDIENTS, AND THE TIME-HONOURED TECHNIQUES THAT ELEVATE EACH DISH TO PERFECTION.

BUT BEYOND THE KITCHEN, THIS COOKBOOK IS A TRIBUTE TO THE SPIRIT OF ITALIAN HOSPITALITY AND THE JOY OF SHARING FOOD WITH LOVED ONES. WHETHER YOU'RE GATHERING AROUND A TABLE WITH FAMILY OR HOSTING A FESTIVE DINNER PARTY WITH FRIENDS, MAY THESE RECIPES INSPIRE MEMORABLE MOMENTS AND FORGE LASTING CONNECTIONS.

AS YOU DELVE INTO THE RECIPES WITHIN THESE PAGES, I ENCOURAGE YOU TO EMBRACE THE ITALIAN PHILOSOPHY OF COOKING WITH PASSION, SAVORING EACH BITE, AND CHERISHING THE COMPANY OF THOSE YOU HOLD DEAR. GRAZIE MILLE!

YOUR FEEDBACK IS GREATLY APPRECIATED!

IT'S THROUGH YOUR FEEDBACK, SUPPORT AND REVIEWS THAT I'M ABLE TO CREATE THE BEST BOOKS POSSIBLE AND SERVE MORE PEOPLE.

I WOULD BE EXTREMELY GRATEFUL IF YOU COULD TAKE JUST 60 SECONDS TO KINDLY LEAVE AN HONEST REVIEW OF THE BOOK ON AMAZON. PLEASE SHARE YOUR FEEDBACK AND THOUGHTS FOR OTHERS TO SEE.

TO DO SO, SIMPLY FIND THE BOOK ON AMAZON'S WEBSITE (OR WHEREVER YOU PURCHASED THE BOOK FROM) AND LOCATE THE SECTION TO LEAVE A REVIEW. SELECT A STAR RATING AND WRITE A COUPLE OF SENTENCES.

THAT'S IT! THANK YOU SO MUCH FOR YOUR SUPPORT.

Review this product

Share your thoughts with other customers

REFERENCES

ASSELIN, M. ITALIAN COCKTAILS: 15 DRINKS RECIPES INSPIRED BY ITALY. HTTPS://FOODNOUVEAU.COM/ITALIAN-COCKTAILS/

ERDEKIAN, A. 11 ITALIAN COCKTAILS YOU CAN MAKE AT HOME. HTTPS://WWW.CNTRAVELER.COM/STORY/ITALIAN-COCKTAILS

D'ARCY, E. WHAT IS A NEGRONI SBAGLIATO WITH PROSECCO IN IT? HTTPS://WWW.BONAPPETIT.COM/STORY/EMMA-DARCY-SBAGLIATO

OVERHISER, S. AMERICANO COCKTAIL HTTPS://WWW.ACOUPLECOOKS.COM/AMERICANO-COCKTAIL/

GRAHAM, C. THE GIN & IT COCKTAIL. HTTPS://WWW.THESPRUCEEATS.COM/GIN-AND-IT-RECIPE-759299

GENTL, A. SALAD OF PINK RADICCHIO, CITRUS, AND MUSHROOM BAGNA CAUDA. HTTPS://WWW.FOODANDWINE.COM/RECIPES/SALAD-OF-PINK-RADICCHIO-CITRUS-AND-MUSHROOM-BAGNA-CAUDA

OLIVER, J. 2005. JAMIE'S ITALY, ANTIPASTI. PUBLISHER: MICHAEL JOSEPH

CARLUCCIO, A & CONTALDO, G. TWO GREEDY ITALIANS EAT ITALY. GAMBERONI E GRANCHIO CON AGLIO E PEPERONCINO. QUADRILLE PUBLISHING

CARLUCCIO, A & CONTALDO, G. TWO GREEDY ITALIANS EAT ITALY. CALAMARI IN UMIDO. QUADRILLE PUBLISHING

OLIVER, J. 69 ANTIPASTI RECIPES. INVOLTINI. HTTPS://WWW.JAMIEOLIVER.COM/RECIPES/CHEESE-RECIPES/INVOLTINI/

OLIVER, J. 69 ANTIPASTI RECIPES. DIY FINGER FOOD. HTTPS://WWW.JAMIEOLIVER.COM/RECIPES/BEEF-RECIPES/DIY-PARTY-COMBOS-BRESAOLA-WITH-MUSTARD-AND-COLESLAW/

TERZINI, M. 2004. SOMETHING ITALIAN. PENGUIN GROUP.

ADAMS, A. BUFFALO MOZZARELLA WITH FIGS, PROSCIUTTO AND HONEY. HTTPS://WWW.TASTE.COM.AU/RECIPES/BUFFALO-MOZZARELLA-FIGS-PROSCIUTTO-HONEY/8C15F1ED-556A-48D2-B829-8D9694128CF1?R=RECIPES/ANTIPASTORECIPES&C=88EBFB3E-A91E-448D-9CBF-D0B724B218ED/ANTIPASTO%20RECIPES

OLIVER, J. GRILLED MUSHROOM RISOTTO. HTTPS://WWW.JAMIEOLIVER.COM/RECIPES/RICE-RECIPES/GRILLED-MUSHROOM-RISOTTO/

OPENAI. (2023). CONVERSATIONS WITH CHATGPT. RETRIEVED 27/10/2023, FROM HTTPS://WWW.OPENAI.COM/CHATGPT/

SAMMAKIEH K. E. FOODIES, TWO GREEDY ITALIANS. HTTPS://WWW.FACEBOOK.COM/FOODIESMAGAZINE1/PHOTOS/A.3 82591051849979/912984728810606/?TYPE=3

CARLUCCIO, A. TWO GREEDY ITALIANS. SLOW COOKED FAMILY STEW WITH POLENTA. HTTPS://WWW.BBC.CO.UK/FOOD/RECIPES/SLOW-COOKED_FAMILY_STEW_33263

BINNS-MACDONALD, C. 2019. PUMPKIN AND SAGE BAKED GNOCCHI. HTTPS://WWW.DELICIOUS.COM.AU/RECIPES/PUMPKIN-SAGE-BAKED-GNOCCHI/OQGUCLZ9?R=RECIPES/COLLECTIONS/OTRCXKHN

OPENAI. (2023). CONVERSATIONS WITH CHATGPT. RETRIEVED 03/11/2023, FROM HTTPS://WWW.OPENAI.COM/CHATGPT/

OPENAI. (2024). CONVERSATIONS WITH CHATGPT. RETRIEVED 08/01/2024, FROM HTTPS://CHAT.OPENAI.COM/C/1A14CF9B-9608-4B7C-953A-AEFA66AC09A5

ITALIAN HOMEMADE 2021. SCALOPPINE AL LIMONE HTTPS://WWW.ITALIANHOMEMADE.CO.UK/POST/SCALOPPINE-AL-LIMONE-SCALOPPINE-WITH-LEMON

SICILIAN GIRL. CHICKEN WITH ROASTED LEMONS, OLIVES & CAPERS. HTTPS://SICILIANGIRL.COM/2020/12/CHICKEN-WITH-ROASTED-LEMONS-OLIVES-CAPERS/

OPENAI. (2024). CONVERSATIONS WITH CHATGPT 3.5. RETRIEVED 19/01/2024. HTTPS://CHAT.OPENAI.COM/C/83629392-7619-4FD9-9275-A19B8A12EB4F

OPENAI. (2024). CONVERSATIONS WITH CHATGPT 3.5. RETRIEVED 19/01/2024. HTTPS://CHAT.OPENAI.COM/C/DADD9D5C-5396-448A-B42A-9E771ADF8A4B

OPENAI. (2024). CONVERSATIONS WITH CHATGPT 3.5. RETRIEVED 19/01/2024. HTTPS://CHAT.OPENAI.COM/C/DEB8B15E-8AFA-4873-9AF7-610259658412

OPENAI. (2024). CONVERSATIONS WITH CHATGPT 3.5. RETRIEVED 19/01/2024. HTTPS://CHAT.OPENAI.COM/C/A33799E0-104C-4E19-A98B-28AB6E3ACD15

OPENAI. (2024). CONVERSATIONS WITH CHATGPT 3.5. RETRIEVED 29/03/2024. HTTPS://CHAT.OPENAI.COM/C/89328B6F-8C56-4524-8FD1-D5EC5E9BB38F

OPENAI. (2024). CONVERSATIONS WITH CHATGPT 3.5. RETRIEVED 29/03/2024. HTTPS://CHAT.OPENAI.COM/C/626F8005-3534-4090-96A4-371CE96868BA

OPENAI. (2024). CONVERSATIONS WITH CHATGPT 3.5. RETRIEVED 29/03/2024. HTTPS://CHAT.OPENAI.COM/C/184A089A-7B75-4C81-B8A9-7E9F7E7AA4E4

OLIVIA MUENTER. 23 NOV 2021. WOMANS DAY. ITALIAN DESSERT RECIPES. THIS LIST OF TRADITIONAL ITALIAN TREATS WILL LEAVE YOU DROOLING. HTTPS://WWW.WOMANSDAY.COM/FOOD-RECIPES/FOOD-DRINKS/RECIPES/A10036/RASPBERRY-RICOTTA-FOOL-121373/

OPENAI. (2024). CONVERSATIONS WITH CHATGPT 3.5. RETRIEVED 29/03/2024. HTTPS://CHAT.OPENAI.COM/C/32D38026-B0F9-441C-B746-C18AEC076A01

www.ingramcontent.com/pod-product-compliance
Lightning Source LLC
Chambersburg PA
CBHW080309030726
47593CB00009B/2696